**PEARS
PUBLISI**

CW00815776

J'apprends le Français:

Student Handbook for
French

Written by Steve Clarke

Cartoons by Steve Clarke

Français

Nom ....

Classe ....

École ....

....

Dates of exams:

1 ....

2 ....

3 ....

Exam board ....

Syllabus numbers ....

Candidate number ....

Centre number ....

Further copies of this publication may be obtained from:

Pearson Publishing
Chesterton Mill, French's Road, Cambridge CB4 3NP
Tel 01223 350555   Fax 01223 356484

Email info@pearson.co.uk   Web site http://www.pearson.co.uk/education/

ISBN: 1 85749 580 2

Published by Pearson Publishing 1999
© Pearson Publishing 1999

Contents

Introduction

This book is not a coursebook. Its purpose is not to teach you all there is to know about learning the French language – your teacher(s) will be doing that. This book is designed to help you out at all those times when the teacher just isn't there, or when he or she needs a few notes to help explain things.

People learn in different ways. The most important factor in determining how successfully you will learn to understand, speak, read and write French is **you**... This book is designed to help you do just that. It will explain what will happen to you as you study French at KS3 and KS4 and it will help you take charge of your learning so that you can make things happen too.

You will find a brief introduction to those things that influence every French teacher but are not always explained to every French student!

1 General advice

Why learn a foreign language?

There is no better way of getting to know about the lives and culture of other people than by talking to them in their own language, and as greater unity is achieved in Europe, there will be less likelihood of never needing to speak a foreign language for personal or for business communication. You will soon be competing for jobs with your European neighbours and, even if you never venture abroad yourself, you are unlikely to work for a company that will not be trading with at least one foreign country. The ability to speak a foreign language is still a good business investment.

All of the following careers give preference to applicants with knowledge of a modern foreign language: Language teacher, translator, travel agent, tourist office worker, air crew, pilot, armed forces, export manager, journalist, tourist guide, interpreter, bilingual/trilingual secretary, hotel/catering manager, wine producer, conference organiser, commodity dealer, civil servant, diplomatic service, fine art/antiques dealer, European law specialist, editorial assistant, export sales engineer, librarian/information scientist.

Ask your Careers Adviser for advice.

She had plans for a high-flying career

Why French?

- French as a foreign language is the second most frequently taught language in the world after English.

- French is spoken as an official language in some 43 countries around the world and is the only language other than English spoken on five continents.

- French, along with English, is the official language of:

  – the United Nations

  – the International Monetary Fund

  – the International Olympic Committee

  – the Council of Europe

  – the European Union.

- French is consistently the preferred foreign language required by the greater number of job adverts.

- French is the second language of the Internet.

- Over 20,000 English words have their origins in the French language.

- France is the world's major tourist destination (approximately 60 million tourists a year).

- French literature boasts some of the most influential writers of modern times.

France remains Britain's closest European neighbour (if you don't count Ireland!) but how many of the world's population speak French, compared to other languages? And which countries are 'Francophone' (French-speaking)?

Table of world languages and number of speakers

Rank	Language	Number of first language speakers
1	Chinese, Mandarin	885,000,000
2	English	322,000,000
3	Spanish	266,000,000
4	Bengali	189,000,000
5	Hindi	182,000,000
6	Portuguese	170,000,000
7	Russian	170,000,000
8	Japanese	125,000,000
9	German	98,000,000
10	Chinese, Wu	77,175,000
11	Javanese	75,500,800
12	Korean	75,000,000
13	French	72,000,000
14	Vietnamese	66,897,000
15	Telugu	66,350,000
24	Polish	44,000,000
27	Italian	40,000,000
37	Romanian	26,000,000
47	Dutch	20,000,000

Bonjour, tout le monde!

French is officially spoken in: France, Belgium, Switzerland, Canada (Québec), Haiti, Monaco, Andorra, Benin, Burkina-Faso, Burundi, Cameroon, Central African Republic, Chad, Comoros, Congo, Côte-d'Ivoire, Djibouti, French Polynesia, Gabon, Guadeloupe, Guinea, Luxembourg, Madagascar, Martinique, Mauritania, Mayotte, New Caledonia, Niger, Reunion, Rwanda, Senegal, Seychelles, St Pierre and Miquelon, Togo, United Kingdom (Channel Islands), Vanuatu, Wallis and Futuna, and Zaire. It is commonly spoken in Mauritius.

2 The National Curriculum

Every school has National Curriculum documents for each subject. These documents describe what teachers should teach at each key stage. For each subject and for each key stage, programmes of study set out what students should be taught and attainment targets set out the expected standards of students' performance:

- Attainment Target 1: Listening and Responding
- Attainment Target 2: Speaking
- Attainment Target 3: Reading and Responding
- Attainment Target 4: Writing

For French, at the end of Key Stage 3, standards of students' performance are set out in eight level descriptions of increasing difficulty, with an additional description above Level 8 for exceptional performance.

To determine which level description matches your performance, look carefully at the descriptions immediately above and below the level you think might apply. If the one below seems too low and the one above seems too high, then the one you are looking at must be... just right!

Pick a level... any level...

A level description can only be decided upon after considering your performance over several tasks, topics or exercises, and you should consider all of your work and not just one or two of your best pieces. What you understand and could do again and again is more important than something you did once... but have since forgotten!

You should be able to get a copy of the National Curriculum level descriptions from your teacher. These have been modified in the 1999 Curriculum Review, so be sure to get the most recent edition.

Once you have worked out which level best describes your current performance, carefully read the next level and look for opportunities to produce evidence of reaching that level. When you know what evidence is needed, you should be working to provide it for your teacher. Remember... it's your progress, not theirs!

Optional tests and tasks at Key Stage 3

At the end of Key Stage 3 (Year 9), your teachers will have to report on your attainment in French. In addition to all the exercises that you will have done in the course of the year, your teachers may use standard tests and tasks designed for this purpose. The optional tests that best fit your performance in a particular attainment target are chosen by your teacher. Optional test and task topics are:

- Unit 1: *Je me présente*
- Unit 2: *Chez moi*
- Unit 3: *Coutumes et traditions*
- Unit 4: *En bonne santé*
- Unit 5: *Où j'habite*
- Unit 6: *Les vacances*
- Unit 7: *L'échange scolaire*
- Unit 8: *La vie de tous les jours*

However, you are more likely to be assessed on your classwork throughout the year, without sitting the National Curriculum optional tests.

CRICCK

The optional tests were designed to stretch even the most able...

3 GCSE examinations

What will I have to do?

Everything you have learnt in French so far, and everything you have yet to learn, is part of your GCSE exam syllabus. Don't make the mistake of thinking that your GCSE doesn't really start until Years 10 and 11. If you think that, you will have missed out on several years of exam practice!

You will be tested in the four Attainment Target skills of Listening, Speaking, Reading and Writing.

How do I know which tier I will sit?

GCSE examinations in French are tiered, and have been since 1998. There are two tiers:

- Foundation Tier
- Higher Tier

Rules of GCSE entry and tiering vary according to the examination board chosen. You should feel confident that your exam entry offers you the best chance of achieving the highest GCSE grade you can realistically expect.

Foundation Tier papers cover the GCSE grades G to C, whilst Higher Tier papers are intended for candidates expecting grades D to A*.

The two tiers overlap which means that the hardest questions of the Foundation Tier reappear as the easiest in the Higher Tier.

GCSE points are awarded according to marks scored: 0 to 5 points are available for Foundation Tier papers; 3 to 8 points are available for Higher Tier papers. Always remember that candidates entered for Higher Tier papers who fail to make the grade will be given 0 points, so there is little point in risking a Higher Tier entry unless you are confident of achieving at least as many GCSE points as those available through Foundation Tier entry.

Obviously, Foundation Tier and Higher Tier vary in their degree of difficulty, but what you have to do is really not very different.

 Listening

With most exam boards, at the start of your French listening exam you will have five minutes to read through the paper with the help of your dictionary. Since 1998, the majority of the questions will be in French and you should use this time to check that you understand exactly what you will have to do for each question.

You will hear the cassette recording that the examination board has provided for your school. The tape will contain conversations, discussions and announcements of varying length from which you will have to extract the required answers. In some cases, you simply tick the correct box, insert a letter or write the number that corresponds to the most appropriate picture, but in others you will need to give your answers in French.

Even though this is the listening exam, you will need to express at least some of your answers in simple phrases that will make sense to the examiner, or indeed to any native French speaker. Not only must you understand the answers, you have to be able to write a little too.

The difference between the Foundation and the Higher Tiers will be the length of the extracts, the complexity of the language, and the difficulty of expressing the inferred answer in French.

Speaking

Unless your teacher has opted for speaking coursework (available through EDEXCEL only), it is quite likely that your first GCSE examination will be your French oral exam. To build your confidence, get off to a flying start!

You need not wait until Year 11 to begin your preparation. If you have to give a short speech or presentation, you can practice that at anytime... even in Year 7! It may not be the speech or presentation that you will give for your final French oral exam, but at least you will have had lots of experience in preparing and presenting such material.

The role-play was going well...

You will have to take part in role-play conversations with role-play cards to guide your conversation. You will have a few minutes to prepare these role-plays, with the help of your dictionary, but be sure that the final GCSE examination is not the first time you see one of these cards. Marks are often lost in the final exam simply by not realising what you have to do or say next.

Most GCSE French oral examinations are recorded and it is important that you are not put off by this. It is recorded for the sole purpose of making it possible to be heard, marked and moderated by more than one person. Practise recording yourself to see how clearly you will be heard and understood.

In a recording lasting little more than 7 to 15 minutes, it is your teacher's job to ensure that the examiner has all the evidence required to award you with a maximum of GCSE points. You need to know what the examiners are expecting to hear.

Whatever examination board you face, you will be judged on:

- Content – stick to the topic and use all the right vocabulary.
- Fluency – avoid lengthy gaps between words and long pauses.
- Independence – be prepared to answer more than the question.
- Pronunciation – try to sound as French as you can.
- Intonation – vary your speed and tone, sound 'surprised' if it says so.
- Use of language – learn to use the expressions that French people use.

In addition, you will be required to express your opinion and show your ability to use a range of tenses.

Take control of your oral and be prepared to answer as fully as you can. Use the time that you might get with a foreign language assistant to develop your confidence, accent, intonation and knowledge of French idioms. Your teacher will tell you the topics that you will need to revise and practise. As soon as you know these, begin to prepare questions and answers relating to the topics.

...Don't be nervous...

Reading

You will be given examples of French texts – cuttings, adverts, postcards, letters, brochures, articles, etc – from which you will have to extract your answers. There will be questions about opening times, details of tours, rules and regulations, definitions and general comprehension. You should make a habit of reading as many examples of such material as you can lay your hands on. Your teachers' cupboards are most likely full of old textbooks that will have examples of GCSE reading material. No matter that the books are old and out of date... the French language will have changed much less than the fashions!

It is a good idea to build your vocabulary by reading French magazines or 'easy-reader' materials. There are often publications that are promoted in schools and you should consider taking advantage of these. Remember the National Curriculum expects you to select French reading material independently, according to your interests.

Who says teachers know nothing about fashion?

 # Writing

If your teacher has chosen the coursework option (available through EDEXCEL, MEG, NEAB and WJEC), you will not have to do a written exam, but the pieces you submit as coursework will decide your GCSE points in this area.

You will have to compile lists, select words to complete short sentences or phrases, compose formal and informal letters and write short narratives. Whatever the task, there is no substitute for a sound knowledge of simple, well-rehearsed, useful phrases. Know how to ask questions, how to

There was more than one way to misuse a dictionary

say something you do, did or will do later. Read the question carefully. For each thing you are asked to write, produce a simple, 'to the point' phrase. Then try to write an additional idea related to it. For example, if you are asked to say 'who you went with', you might put: *Je suis allé(e) avec mon copain.* Then you can add, *Il s'appelle Tom et il est très amusant.* A second additional phrase each time will build your response into a good example of written French likely to get good marks. Don't make things too complicated and be sure that whenever you need to look up a word in your dictionary, you know how to choose the correct meaning. Examiners have laughed themselves silly over some of the expressions they have read as a result of dictionary misuse.

Sharon always used some of her revision time for filing...

Select pieces of writing that you have done in class or at home and file these away for revision. You are more likely to remember words and phrases that apply to your own particular circumstances.

11

Reports on the GCSE examination frequently refer to the difficulty students have in asking simple questions. If you can add this skill to your repertoire, you will be at an advantage in the French writing exam. You need only learn a few basic structures to cover the vast majority of possible questions you might need to write. Commit these to memory and be sure that you can use them in both the *Tu* form (talking to a friend) and the *Vous* form (talking to more than one friend, talking to someone you have not met or ought to respect).

Your teacher can provide you with a list of the GCSE topics. With this list in mind, you will be able to prepare letters and reports covering the most likely GCSE tasks. (See page 77 for National Curriculum Areas of Experience.)

In addition, you should memorise a suitable start and end for both an informal letter to a friend and a more formal business letter. You are bound to need one or the other in your final exam, and maybe even both.

Writing coursework

Most of the examining groups require that you submit three pieces of written coursework – SEG is the exception and requires only two. Of these three, two may be done at home but at least one must be done under controlled conditions. Teachers usually insist on more than the minimum number of written pieces required for coursework so that they can select and submit your best efforts for your final mark. Whatever your teacher's choice, your coursework will be typically approached as follows:

- Task training – Your teacher will present a topic or unit of work and let you know that it provides an opportunity for a piece of coursework.

- Discussion of task choice – Your teacher will ask you to choose a task or a title and expect you to talk through how best to present your answer.

- Discussion of first draft or outline – Your teacher will read through your work and recommend improvements, so the better your work, the more likely you are to get useful comments.

- Production of the final piece – You should rewrite your first draft after checking all the things that your teacher has recommended.

- Certificate of authenticity – You will be asked to sign a statement that your piece of work is your own unaided effort. Your teacher will have to countersign this statement.

The teacher's initial reaction to the certificate of authenticity was not promising...

Coursework tasks vary from examining group to group and your teacher will advise you on how to approach the titles and topics.

When do I start to prepare for my GCSE?

Since every word and phrase you learn in French can be used in the GCSE examinations, you should start preparing for the final exam **now**! As early as Year 7 (Year 6 in some cases), you will be taught parts of the GCSE French syllabus. Make sure you learn them all thoroughly and take the time to rehearse them as often as you can.

I'm not in Year 11, I can't answer that!

13

How do I learn new vocabulary?

Set yourself realistic targets for each year of your French studies. An analysis of the syllabus shows that the French GCSE exam demands a core vocabulary of 1458 words. Given that a typical GCSE course is 140 hours, then the amount of vocabulary that has to be learnt or revised per lesson is 11 words. If you make a good start on building up your French vocabulary in Years 7, 8 and 9 you will extend the number of hours to something like 360 hours – that's only four words a lesson!

You can improve your ability to learn vocabulary with regular practice. Develop the habit of learning every lesson's vocabulary.

I've learnt four words... I'm off!

There are lots of methods used by lots of people to learn new things. Explore all the possibilities and don't be afraid to ask what methods others have used. The following techniques may be useful to start your research off:

- **Vocabulary lists:** Make a list of French words and their English meaning. Cut a 'testing' card, as shown, and use it to cover the French words as you go down the list, you can check your answers as they are revealed. By turning the card over, you can cover the English to test yourself in reverse.

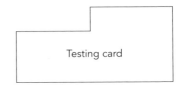

Testing card

- **Grouping vocabulary by topic:** Try learning words related to one topic rather than just a lot of words that happen to start with the same letter of the alphabet.

- **Linking vocabulary by a short story:** Try to invent an imaginary story that uses all the words you are trying to learn. As you recall the story, you will find it easier to remember the related vocabulary too.

- **Word association:** Some words suggest English words, phrases or images that may help you remember French words. For example, to remember the spelling of *beau*, you might use '**B**ig **E**lephants **A**re **U**gly'.

- **Mini flash-cards:** You can make your own set of cards to test your vocabulary. They might have pictures on one side and the French word on the reverse, or simply the French word on one side and the English on the other.

- **Elimination game:** Put all the words you need to learn into a small box (after dinner mint boxes are ideal for this). As you go through trying to remember the French words, remove all the cards that you get right first time and leave any others in the box for the next time. As you go through the box, over and over again, you will find yourself concentrating on the words you don't know very well, rather than wasting time on the ones that you know already.

Somebody had to provide the chocolate boxes, he explained!

Always write down the vocabulary you are learning. Words that sound the same can be written in several ways in French (*manger, mangé, mangeais*). Be sure you know the difference.

If you decide to work with a partner to make things more fun, be sure that you are both learning the vocabulary you need. It won't be much use in the examination if your friend knows all the words but you don't!

Revisit past topics and vocabulary frequently. There's not much point learning lots of words one week if you are going to forget them all the next. A little and often is better than a lot once or twice. If you wait until the day before the exam and try to learn the 1500 words needed, you are not likely to succeed.

Language learning skills

Each of the Attainment Target skills will be tested and will be awarded 25% of your final GCSE marks, so it is worth thinking about how to improve your performance in all four areas. Establish good habits at an early stage:

Listening – Start by resolving never to talk during a listening exercise. Sooner or later you will have to answer the question on your own and it is best to get into the habit early. If you understand enough to answer the question, then don't be put off by all the bits you didn't understand. This is part of the learning process. Practise listening to the words and structures that you meet in class as often as you can. Make the most of the role-play and pair-work exercises that you will do every year so that you practise listening to others as well as learning to say your part.

Speaking – Listen carefully to how words and phrases sound and try your best to say them correctly. Record yourself frequently and play it back. You will hear what you need to improve. Don't be afraid of making mistakes – there are times when getting your message across is more important than getting it exactly right. Remember that French is a language – you should be able to vary your intonation as much as you do in your own mother tongue. Ask your teacher or the foreign language assistant to record some short dialogues for you to practise. The GCSE examination rewards good intonation, pronunciation, accuracy, fluency and independence... keep these words in mind when you speak.

Reading – Get into the habit of reading French. Find out about French readers, supplementary magazines, Internet resources, pen-pal letter-writing opportunities and any other reading material that you can. If you are lucky enough to go to, or through, France for a holiday, take a notebook to note words from signs and posters. You can buy teen magazines in most newsagents or at the local *Tabac*. Keeping your own vocabulary notebook can be a really good way of helping you revisit and revise the words that you come across as you read. Try not to be too worried about understanding every word if you are able to understand the gist of a message or text.

Be selective in the words that you decide to memorise... some words are very interesting but are not very useful in other contexts. Learn words and phrases that are useful in a whole range of situations. *Je voudrais...* (I would like...) could be used to start a conversation in any number of places or situations. Learn useful words and phrases thoroughly. You can always look up words if you need to, but it is a waste of time to have to keep looking up simple questions or expressions that you will meet often.

Can we go there one day, mum?

Writing – Start by learning to copy words correctly and practise spelling them accurately. Compile and rehearse lists of vocabulary that you come across in the classroom. Even if your teacher doesn't insist, take time to learn whether a new French word is masculine or feminine – should it start with *un* or *une*?, *le* or *la*?, or is it plural? If it is, how do I know if it is masculine or feminine? These details become more and more important as you progress in French and it makes sense to start by getting such details sorted out. If these details are a real problem for you, concentrate on the words themselves first and worry about the details later.

The GCSE emphasises the ability to make yourself understood first and foremost, and rewards details of accuracy afterwards. If you never get to writing French accurately, at least you can get marks by making yourself understood. If

He doesn't seem to understand his own language!

your writing is really difficult to read, practise your handwriting... writing slowly, with a pen, and making your letters larger than usual, often helps. Remember, that in the GCSE exam your writing skills will be needed to answer questions in the listening and reading papers as well as the writing. You will need to write simple phrases to answer some of the more advanced questions. Practise writing letters often.

Within every topic that you learn, take time to memorise useful expressions that you might include in a letter and practise their spelling. Be sure you can write such phrases from memory. Take time to look at what you, or others, have written. Consider why certain words are used or omitted. Begin to understand which part of what you have written carries what meaning. Learn to apply the rules of grammar that you have had explained in class and take time to proofread your writing. Look out for mistakes with adjectives, tenses or accents.

If you turn to the section about French handwriting on page 115, you will learn a clever way of producing accents so as to disguise the fact that you can't remember if they go one way or the other.

Deciding on a GCSE grade to work towards

Read the next section, 'How will they work out my grade?' and decide which grade you would like to get at GCSE. Plan your progress toward obtaining that grade. You are more likely to achieve your aims if they are fully understood and you have mapped out the steps of progression along the way.

The real difference between a high GCSE grade and a mediocre one is linguistic competence, which comes as much through thorough preparation as from natural ability. Being prepared for GCSE examinations in French will improve your performance and, consequently, your grade.

Typical grade descriptions for each Attainment Target skill are listed in each exam syllabus. These descriptions of performance outline the standards of achievement likely to have been shown by candidates who were awarded particular grades. Descriptions are included for Grades F, C and A. You can assume that the other grades will be either more or less demanding – those gaining a grade G will be less competent that those gaining a grade F, and those obtaining a grade A* will naturally be more competent than those awarded grade A.

How will they work out my grade?

Candidates achieve their grade by obtaining sufficient GCSE points according to the following scale:

Points total	GCSE grade awarded
30-32	A*
25-29	A
21-24	B
16-20	C
12-15	D
8-11	E
5-7	F
2-4	G
0-1	U

Your score in each French exam will be awarded GCSE points and the total number of points, irrespective of which tier you sat in each paper, will be converted to a GCSE grade. Your teacher will be able to tell you the 'score to points' ratio for the exam papers you will practise. These vary from year to year. Full GCSE points does not require 100% accuracy so you can afford a few mistakes.

Did I show you my grade? he said...again...and again...and...

4 Grammar

Teachers have varying views about grammar and they do not all agree about how to teach it. Yet without it – without any sense of pattern – a foreign language is just a muddle of unpredictable words that would have to be remembered in isolation.

Grammar is undoubtedly important and you could not hope to progress very far in learning French without some level of grammatical understanding. The question is... how is the grammar taught? – or, more importantly, how is it learned?

Often the problem is not understanding the grammar, itself, but the words used to explain it. For many students, learning French grammar can be like learning two languages... French and the language of grammar.

There must be a balance. You must be prepared to be spontaneous when the situation demands, and able to think through the application of grammatical patterns and rules when the need arises.

Whilst there is nothing wrong with using correct grammatical terms, you should not feel that you need to explain every language structure that you use... just be happy to use it. It is easier, in some cases, just to learn the phrase without the explanation.

Spontaneous... or accurate?!

Teachers of French often prefer to emphasise the recognition of language patterns rather than the strict application of rules. Textbooks often have little charts presenting such language patterns to be used as a model for producing accurate language, but these do not teach you where exactly words that are not on the chart fit into the pattern. For this you will need to know the rules that created the pattern in the first place.

Make up your mind that you will not be the type of student that gets bogged down with working out the rules at the cost of uninhibited communication, nor will you be the type of student who communicates happily without ever bothering about accuracy. The best kind of student to be is one who can use the rules in situations where accuracy is appropriate, but is not afraid of making minor mistakes in the interests of communication.

Look out for language rules and patterns that are presented and learn them thoroughly. Something that does not look very important when you first meet it may well turn out to be an essential part of a far more complicated structure that needs to be tackled later on.

The material within this section aims to provide a reference for the main points of French grammar. Each explanation is followed by some simple exercises that you can do to prove that you understand the basic workings of the grammatical point you have been revising. The answers to the exercises are provided at the back of the book. Try not to look at them until you have completed all the questions in the exercise.

If you find a particular exercise very difficult, and you are still unsure about the grammatical rules, then you will know what to ask your teacher to help you with. There is no point simply ignoring it and hoping it will go away. Your lack of understanding may go undetected all the way to the examination room, but it will certainly be exposed there! Don't be afraid to ask.

She had coped well with the exams pressure... until now!

Glossary of grammatical terms

What do all the words mean?

There are many grammatical terms that you may come across, but a thorough knowledge of the ones listed here will be more than enough to help you through Years 7 to 11 and they will help bridge the 'grammar gap' between GCSE and A-level French.

Adjective	'Describing word', a word describing a noun or pronoun. Examples: big, blue, interesting, strange.
Adverb	'Describes' a verb, giving information on how something is done. Examples: slowly, quietly, angrily.
Agreement	Adjectives in French sometimes alter their spelling to agree with, or 'match', the noun they describe. Masculine nouns need masculine adjective spelling, feminine nouns need feminine adjective spelling, and plural nouns need to be either masculine or feminine and plural. Examples: *un pantalon vert, une jupe verte, des chaussettes vertes.* (Past participles, see page 59, used like adjectives have to 'agree' too) *Il est allé, Elle est allée, Ils sont allés, Elles sont allées.*
Articles	There are three sorts of article:

- definite   *le, la, les* (the)
- indefinite   *un, une* (a)
- partitive   *du, de la, des* (some).

Comparatives	Adjectives and adverbs used to compare things. Examples: smaller, larger, faster.
Conjugation	The pattern that verbs follow. Regular verbs in French belong to the *-er, -ir* and *-re* conjugations, but not all verbs follow the rules. Verbs that do are called regular verbs, the ones that do not are irregular verbs.

Conjunction   Words used to join clauses or sentences. Examples: and, because, for.

Gender   Every noun in French is either masculine or feminine, *un* or *une*, *le* or *la*. The rules are generally based on the spelling of the noun and not on the noun itself, so a bicycle may be called, *un vélo* (masculine) or *une bicyclette* (feminine).

Imperatives   Command forms of verbs used to give orders, 'Let's...'

Examples: *Écoute!*   (Listen!)
    Écoutez!   (Listen!)
    Écoutons!   (Let's listen!).

Infinitive   The verb without a subject. How it appears in the dictionary or on a vocabulary list. In English, they always start with the word 'to...' Examples: *manger* (to eat), *être* (to be).

Interrogative pronouns   Words used to ask the question 'Who?' or 'What?'.

Nouns   'Naming' words: places, people, things. Examples: Mum, Dad, cat, dog, soldier, courage.

Object   Whatever is affected by the action of a verb. Examples: I watch **television**, I like **it**.

You will need to know the difference between a direct and an indirect object (see pages 32 to 35).

Past participle   How the verb looks and sounds in the past. Some are used with *avoir* and others with *être*. Be sure to follow rules about agreement. Examples: *J'ai mangé*, *Je suis allé(e)*.

Prepositions   Placed before nouns and pronouns to show position and other relationships. Example: in, on, at, under, beside, etc.

Pronoun	Words used instead of a noun, often to avoid repetition. Examples: he, she, I, it.
Relative pronouns	Introduce a clause giving more information about a noun. Example: the man **that** I saw.
Subject	This is the person or thing that is 'doing' the verb. Examples: I, you, he, she, the man.
Tenses	These are the different forms of the verb that give information about when something takes place, took place or will take place.
Verb	This is often said to be a 'doing' word, ie what someone or something is 'doing', but it also includes verbs like to be, which really aren't 'doing' anything! Examples: she **watches** TV, the cat **is** on the mat.

1 Nouns

Can you tell which words are nouns?

A noun is a 'naming' word. It might help to imagine a Christmas present list... if the word you are thinking of is something you might wish to give or get for Christmas, then it is a noun. This includes things that you cannot see or touch, like peace, love or happiness.

 ### Exercise A

Which of these French words are nouns?

1 *trois* ☐	4 *chat* ☐	7 *petit* ☐	10 *table* ☐
2 *au revoir* ☐	5 *mère* ☐	8 *livre* ☐	11 *crayon* ☐
3 *stylo* ☐	6 *gomme* ☐	9 *silence* ☐	12 *habite* ☐

Masculine or feminine? How to say 'the' – *le, la, l', les*

In French, all nouns are either masculine or feminine. This is easy to work out when the noun refers to a person, but how does anyone decide about words like 'pencil' or 'book'? There are a few basic rules, or rather clues, that will point you in the right direction, but the only sure way is to use your dictionary to check. When you look up a French word in the dictionary, it will tell you whether or not that word is a noun (n), and whether it is masculine (m) or feminine (f). So you will see an entry that looks something like this – '*maison* -nf. house' or 'house - n. *maison* f.'

	the
Masculine	*le*
Feminine	*la*
Before a vowel (or silent 'h')	*l'*
Plural	*les*

Clues for recognising the gender of a noun:

Nouns which are masculine	Nouns which are feminine
Male family members/relatives	Female family members/relatives
Job titles relating to men	Job titles relating to women
Countries not ending in -e	Countries and regions ending in -e
Fruit and vegetables not ending in -e	Fruit and vegetables ending in -e (exception: *le pamplemousse*)
Days, months, seasons	Shops ending in -e
Languages	Nouns ending in -*ion*
Most words adopted from English	Nouns ending in -*té*
Nouns ending in -c	Nouns ending in -*ette*
Nouns ending in -*age*	

*This was possibly a clue for
recognising gender...*

Exercise B

Find the correct word for 'the' (*le, la, l'* or *les*), for each noun:

1 ....*samedi*	4 ....*tomate*	7 ....*football*	10 ....*natation*
2 ....*lac*	5 ....*France*	8 ....*sac*	11 ....*française*
3 ....*Canada*	6 ....*pâtisserie*	9 ....*pommes*	12 ....*école*

Masculine, feminine – How to say 'a'

Just as there are different words for 'the' in French, there are two different words for 'a':

	a
Masculine	un
Feminine	une

 ### Exercise C

Write out these nouns using *un* or *une*:

1 ...... *trousse*   4 ...... *chat*   7 ...... *serviette*   10 ...... *table*

2 ...... *tee-shirt*   5 ...... *veste*   8 ...... *jupe*   11 ...... *crayon*

3 ...... *stylo*   6 ...... *gomme*   9 ...... *chien*   12 ...... *jour*

Plural nouns – How to say 'some'

In English, the plural of 'a' is 'some'. In French, the plural of *un* or *une* is *des*. You will always need to add the little word *des* when listing items. In English you can say, 'We have apples and bananas', but in French, you will need to say, *Nous avons des pommes et des bananes*.

Most French and English words form their plural by adding -s. But, just as some English words do not follow this pattern – foot/feet, woman/women, sheep/sheep, mouse/mice – so, there are a few French words that change the spelling of the plural noun. This table will help:

Words which...	... change like this
end in -al	end in -aux
end in -au, -eau, -ou or -eu	add -x
already end in -s, -x or -z	do not change

 ### Exercise D

Write out these nouns using *des*:

1 *journal*   3 *neveu*   5 *nez*   7 *table*

2 *cheval*   4 *eau*   6 *prix*   8 *crayon*

How to say 'some' when you want a quantity

There are times you will say 'some' when you are not talking about more than one thing; some sugar, some cheese, some lemonade, some wine. In all of these examples, you are only talking about 'part' of something. For this reason the partitive article is required. In French, this is made up of the word *de* followed by *le*, *la* or *l'*. But, the spelling of *de + le* becomes *du*:

			some
Masculine	de + le	=	du
	de + l'	=	de l'
Feminine	de + la	=	de la
	de + l'	=	de l'

In English, we sometimes miss out the word 'some', eg 'I'd like bread, cheese and flour', but in French you must always use it, eg *Je voudrais du pain, du fromage et de la farine.*

 Exercise E

Ask for these items using 'Je voudrais ...' with *du*, *de la* or *de l'*:

1 *limonade*	4 *vin*	7 *chocolat*	10 *pizza*
2 *yaourt*	5 *café*	8 *lait*	11 *eau*
3 *pain*	6 *fromage*	9 *confiture*	12 *tarte*

De – in a negative sentence

In English, we change the word 'some' to 'any' when we use a negative, eg 'I have some cheese' but 'I don't have any eggs'. In French, the word *de* is always used without adding an extra *le*, *la* or *l'*.

 Exercise F

Complete this list of things you don't eat using, *Je ne mange pas...*:

1 *bonbons*	3 *viande*	5 *chocolat*	7 *pizza*
2 *yaourt*	4 *poisson*	6 *soupe*	8 *riz*

2 Pronouns

A pronoun is a word that stands in for a noun. For example, instead of saying 'Mr Smith' you can say 'he', instead of saying 'Mum' you can say 'she', and instead of 'my Dad and I', you can say 'we'. Pronouns come in different types.

Subject pronouns

The subject of a verb is the person or thing 'doing' the verb. So a subject pronoun is the word that is used to refer to this thing or person. In English, we use: I, you, he, she, it, we, they – followed by a verb. In French, the words are: *je, tu, il, elle, on, nous, vous, ils* and *elles*.

		English	French
Singular	1st person	I	*je (j')*
	2nd person	you	*tu*
	3rd person	he	*il*
		she	*elle*
		one	*on*
Plural	1st person	we	*nous*
	2nd person	you	*vous*
	3rd person	they (masculine)	*ils*
		they (feminine)	*elles*

'*Tu*' or '*vous*'?

In English, we only have one word for 'you'; the French have two. The first, *tu*, is used only when talking to one person at a time, and only if that person is a member of your family, a good friend, someone about your age who is expected to be your friend, or an animal. *Vous* is used to talk to more than one person at the same time or to someone you have never met, who is older than you and who deserves your respect.

I have a schizophrenic goldfish, is that 'tu' or 'vous'?

 Exercise A

Would you use '*tu*' or '*vous*' when speaking to these?

1 Mum	3 Granny	5 Policeman	7 Teacher
2 Shopkeeper	4 Parents	6 Friend	8 Cat

'*Ils*' or '*Elles*'?

A group need only have one part that is masculine to make the whole group masculine so, for example, a group of 2,000,000 girls and one boy is masculine.

Exercise B

Would you use '*ils*' or '*elles*' when speaking of these?

1 *mes parents*	4 *mes soeurs*	7 *les français*	10 *les profs*
2 *les filles*	5 *mes copines*	8 *les pommes*	11 *les chiens*
3 *les femmes*	6 *les hommes*	9 *les cours*	12 *mes amis*

'*Il*' or '*Elle*'?

In English we use the words 'he' and 'she' only when talking of people, and the word 'it' for anything else. In French, since every noun is either masculine or feminine, the words *il* or *elle* are used rather than any other word that might mean 'it'. So you might say, *J'aime ma chambre.* **Elle** *est grande.* or *J'aime mon vélo.* **Il** *est super.*

It's a boy!

'*Nous*' or '*on*'?

In English, you would probably think someone rather 'posh' if they said things like, 'One likes to go to the cinema'. In French, however, *on*, is used in the same way as 'one' without you sounding posh. It is commonly used instead of *nous*. *On* always uses the same part of the verb as *il* or *elle* and is therefore much easier to say and quicker to write.

 **Exercise C**

Change these sentences from *on* to *nous* and vice-versa:

1 *Nous allons au café*   4 *Nous pouvons entrer?*

2 *Ici, on parle français*   5 *On va à la plage*

3 *Nous mangeons beaucoup*   6 *On va bientôt arriver*

Me, you, him, her, it, us, them

This small group of words in English can be translated in three different ways in French, depending on what type of pronoun is being used. This same group of words can be:

- direct object pronouns
- indirect object pronouns
- emphatic pronouns.

You will only know which pronoun to use if you can recognise which is which.

Direct object pronouns

Remember that the direct object is the person or thing to which the verb is being 'done'.

 Exercise D

Can you identify the direct object in these sentences?

1 She saw me.   3 He stroked the cat.   5 We bought a car.

2 They hit her.   4 She ate an apple.   6 I can see you.

In French, the direct object pronouns are: *me, te, le, la, nous, vous, les*:

	English	French
Singular	me	*me**
	you	*te**
	him/it	*le**
	her/it	*la**
Plural	us	*nous*
	you	*vous*
	them	*les*

* *me, te, le* and *la* become *m', t'* or *l'* before a vowel or a silent *h*

The direct object pronoun is always placed before the verb. Or, in the case of verbs requiring the use of *avoir* or *être*, before the part of *avoir* or *être* that is used. Whenever the direct object precedes (comes before) a past participle, the verb must 'agree' with the preceding direct object: ie *je l'ai vu* (masculine), but *je l'ai vue* (feminine).

 Exercise E

Can you put the pronoun in the French translation of each sentence?

1 He sees him.
Il ..... voit.

2 I like him.
Je .... aime.

3 She sees him.
Elle ..... voit.

4 He finds me.
Il ..... trouve.

5 I'm looking for her.
Je .... cherche.

6 They find us.
Ils ..... trouvent.

 Exercise F

Complete these sentences with the correct French pronoun:

1 *J'aime bien ce tee-shirt, je ..... achète.* (it)

2 *Je n'aime pas les oignons, je ne ..... mange pas.* (them)

3 *Où es Marie? Je ne ..... voit plus.* (her)

4 *Tu .... écoutes?* (me)

5 *Il a des baskets neuves, il ..... porte tout le temps.* (them)

Indirect object pronouns

An indirect object pronoun is not the person or thing to which the verb is being 'done', but it is the person or thing affected subsequently by the action of the verb.

In English, the indirect object pronouns are the same as the direct object pronouns we have just met: me, you, him, her, it, us, them. The only way to tell them apart in English is to decide whether the word 'to' appears or could appear in front of them. For example, 'I gave her the book', could be written 'I gave the book to her'. If you can insert the word 'to', then the pronoun must be an indirect object pronoun. (For the verb 'to buy', you will need to insert 'for'.)

 ### Exercise G

Can you identify the indirect object in these English sentences?

1 I gave her my diary.

2 They bought him a bicycle.

3 Granny gave me some socks.

4 Did you buy him a present?

5 She sent me a letter.

6 He told them a story.

7 Mum gave them an apple.

8 We sent you a postcard.

In French, the indirect pronouns are: *me, te, lui, nous, vous, leur.*

	English	French
	English	**French**
Singular	(to) me	*me**
	(to) you	*te**
	(to) him/her/it	*lui*
Plural	(to) us	*nous*
	(to) you	*vous*
	(to) them	*leur*

* *me* and *te* become *m'* and *t'* before a vowel or a silent *h*

You will notice that most of these are the same as the French direct object pronouns only *lui* and *leur* are different.

 **Exercise H**

Can you complete these sentences filling in the missing pronouns?

1 *Il ..... donne son sac.* (to her)   4 *Je ..... ai écrit.* (to you)

2 *Tu ..... prêtes ton stylo?* (to me)   5 *Il ..... a parlé.* (to them)

3 *Vous ..... donnez le livre.* (to us) 6 *On ..... a écrit.* (to him)

Direct and indirect pronouns together

You will need to identify these two different types of pronouns as they often appear in the same sentence. For example, 'I give it to her' has them both; 'it' is the direct object pronoun and 'to her' is the indirect object pronoun.

 Exercise I

Can you identify which are the direct or indirect pronouns?

1 I gave it to him.   4 She sent me a postcard.

2 We told them a short story.   5 I wrote you a letter.

3 My Dad sold him a car.   6 They gave him a tie-pin.

In French, indirect object pronouns, like direct object pronouns, are placed before the verb or, in the case of a past participle with *avoir* or *être*, before the part of *avoir* or *être* that is used. Since both types of pronoun need to be put in the same place, you will need to know the correct order whenever both appear in the same sentence. This diagram will help:

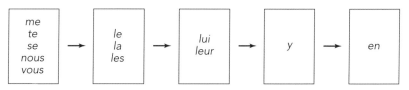

Use the pronouns in the order they appear on the chart from left to right

35

Exercise J

Put the extra pronouns into these sentences in the correct order:

1 *Marie me prête.* (+ *les*)   4 *Je te donne.* (+ *la*)

2 *Vous achetez.* (+ *les* + *nous*)   5 *Elle la donne.* (+ *leur*)

3 *Le prof lui donne.* (+ *les*)   6 *Papa les achète.* (+ *vous*)

 Exercise K

Write the sentences in *italics*, in French, using pronouns:

1 She sends John the letter. *She sends it to him.*

2 Alain and I buy Granny a present. *We buy it for her.*

3 I bought her a T-shirt. *I bought it for her.*

4 We gave them the tickets. *We gave them to them.*

Emphatic pronouns

When you want to use the words,
me, you, him, her, us, you or them,
to emphasise who you are talking
about, or whenever you use these
words on their own to answer a
question, then you are using them
as emphatic pronouns – that is,
pronouns that add emphasis. In
French, this set of words translates as:

*He was emphatically refusing
to do his pronoun homework*

	English	French
Singular	me	*moi*
	you	*toi*
	him	*lui*
	her	*elle*
Plural	us	*nous*
	you	*vous*
	them (masculine)	*eux*
	them (feminine)	*elles*

These words apply only to people or animals and are used:

- to add emphasis ... *Moi, j'ai 12 ans, et lui, il a 14 ans.*
- on their own in single word answers ... *Qui? Moi*
- after prepositions (see page 72) ... *C'est <u>pour</u> Toi*

 ## Exercise L

Replace the people <u>underlined</u> with the right emphatic pronoun:

1 *Marie est allée avec <u>son frère</u>.*   4 *Vous allez avec <u>Marc</u>.*

2 *Il mange avec <u>ma mère et moi</u>.*   5 *Je l'ai acheté pour <u>Paul et Tom</u>.*

3 *Jean est parti sans <u>son amie</u>.*   6 *Tu manges avec <u>les filles</u>.*

You can use these emphatic pronouns after the word *à* when you need to say that something belongs to someone – *C'est à moi* or *le sac est à lui*.

Interrogative pronouns

These are simply words that are used to ask the question 'Who?' or 'What?'. This table will help you get your questions off to a good start:

To...	meaning	use...
ask about a person	Who?	*qui?*
ask about a thing	What?	*que or qu'est ce que ...?**

* If instead of *qu'est ce que?* you use only *que ...?*, you must swap the verb and the subject round immediately after it.

 ## Exercise M

Start these questions with the correct interrogative pronoun:

1 ..... *parle français?*

2 ..... *fais-tu le weekend?*

3 ..... *va au cinéma ce soir?*

4 ..... *veux-tu faire?*

5 ..... *fait la cuisine?*

6 ..... *tu veux regarder?*

It turned out to be an interrogative pronoun

Relative pronouns

Relative pronouns introduce a clause giving more information about a noun. You will need to be confident of identifying whether the relative pronoun is used as the subject of the clause, the direct object, or the indirect object of the clause. The following examples will help:

Relative pronoun used as the subject of the clause (ie **qui**):

- *L'homme **qui** est arrivé est mon père.*
- *Le train **qui** va à Paris va bientôt arriver.*
- *Les enfants **qui** jouent dans le jardin.*

Relative pronoun used as the direct object of the clause (ie **que**):

- *Le film **que** nous avons vu.*
- *La matière **que** j'aime le mieux... c'est le français!*
- *La fille **que** tu cherches est partie.*

If there was one thing worse than a relative pronoun...

Relative pronoun used as the indirect object of the clause (ie **á qui**):

- *L'homme **à qui** j'ai donné les clés.*

Relative pronoun expressing 'whose', 'of whom' or 'of which' (ie **dont**):

- *L'argent **dont** j'ai besoin.*
- *Voilà la fille **dont** je parle.*
- *L'homme **dont** le chien est mort.*

it was a relative pronoun with photos!

Relative pronoun after prepositions – **lequel, laquelle, lesquels, lesquelles** (which):

- *Voici le revolver avec **lequel** M. Moutard a tué M. X*
- *La voiture dans **laquelle** je l'ai vu.*
- *Les raisons pour **lesquelles** il est parti.*

Exercise N

Can you insert the right relative pronoun?

1 *Les films ..... tu adores.*

2 *La fille ..... sort avec Paul.*

3 *L'homme ..... nous regarde.*

4 *Le thé ...... boit ma mère.*

5 *La fille ..... fume.*

6 *Le chien ..... m'a mordu.*

'Y' and 'en' and other pronouns

Y and *en* are commonly used pronouns. This table will help you decide when to use them:

When you have...	Example
y expressing location (there)	*J'y vais*
y replacing *à* (at, in it/them)	*J'y crois*
en replacing *du, de la, des* (some, any, of it/them)	*J'en ai beaucoup*
en replacing *de* in expressions of quantity (of it/them)	*J'en ai trouvé deux*

Exercise O

Replace the words underlined by '*y*' or '*en*':

1 *Je vais au collège.*

2 *Tu veux encore du pain?*

3 *Mon père travaille au stade.*

4 *Il a deux lapins.*

5 *Nous sommes à la gare.*

6 *Paul m'a parlé du voyage.*

There are a few other words known as 'indefinite pronouns'. There really aren't any rules to learn about these words but, since there are not many of them, it is probably best to learn them as vocabulary.

Indefinite pronoun	Example
autre	*Je n'ai pas vu Paul, mais j'ai vu les autres.*
chacun	*Il a beaucoup d'amis, chacun est sympa.*
n'importe	*N'importe qui, n'importe quoi.*

plusieurs	*A-t-il des amis? Oui, il en a plusieurs.*
quelqu'un	*J'attends quelqu'un.*
tous	*Elle était aimée de tous.*
tout	*Maintenant tu sais tout.*
tout le monde	*J'invite tout le monde.*

3 Adjectives

Can you identify which words are adjectives?

Adjectives are 'describing' words. They 'describe' a noun. They tell you what the noun is like.

 Exercise A

Can you identify all the adjectives in these English sentences?

1 The weather is fine.
2 I hate noisy children!
3 It was a little house.
4 Everyone was tired.

5 All they had was cold soup.
6 The big, black cat.
7 He was nice, but a bit shy.
8 French is easy.

The position of adjectives – before or after the noun?

Although most adjectives come after the noun in French, some adjectives do come in front of the noun, just as in English. The most common adjectives which come in front of the noun are:

petit	small	*mauvais*	bad
grand	big/tall	*gros*	big/fat
beau	beautiful	*long*	long
joli	pretty	*haut*	high
bon	good	*vieux*	old

This means you may well read and write sentences with an adjective on either side of the noun – one in front and one after.

Exercise B

Can you correctly place these adjectives into the sentence?

1 *Une fille (jolie)* 6 *Un voyage (long)*
2 *Un élève (bon)* 7 *Un prof (mauvais)*
3 *Un village (joli, petit)* 8 *Des chaussettes (blanches)*
4 *Un lapin (petit, noir)* 9 *Une idée (bonne)*
5 *Une maison (moderne)* 10 *Une dame (vieille)*

You will need to be careful with the placing of some adjectives which have two completely different meanings depending on their position before or after the noun:

mon cher ami	my dear friend
un pull cher	an expensive jumper
un seul garçon	only one boy
un garçon seul	a lonely boy
une famille pauvre	a poor family
le pauvre petit	the poor little boy
un ancien ami	a former friend
un village ancien	an ancient village
ma propre chambre	my own room
une chambre propre	a clean room

 Exercise C

Can you place the adjective so that it makes sense?

1 *Je l'ai fait de mes ...... mains ...... (propres)*
2 *C'est la ..... solution ...... (seule)*
3 *Il y a une réunion pour des ...... élèves ...... (anciens)*
4 *Un ...... pull ...... en laine. (cher)*
5 *Les ...... gens ...... n'ont pas beaucoup d'argent. (pauvres)*

Agreement of adjectives – masculine, feminine, plural

Since all nouns in French are either masculine or feminine, singular or plural, all adjectives have to 'agree' with the noun they refer to. This means that a masculine noun needs a masculine adjective, a feminine noun needs a feminine adjective, and so on.

To make most adjectives feminine you need only add an -e.

Masculine	Feminine	Meaning
petit	petite	small
grand	grande	big, tall
content	contente	happy
fatigué	fatiguée	tired
froid	froide	cold
chaud	chaude	hot
noir	noire	black
joli	jolie	pretty

Those adjectives that already end with the letter -e do not change.

Exercise D

Copy these sentences choosing the correctly spelt adjective:

1   Virginie est (grand/grande).
2   Le sac est (lourd/lourde).
3   Ma mère est très (joli/jolie).
4   Un enfant (bruyant/bruyante).
5   Elle est (branché/branchée).
6   Une (petit/petite) ville.
7   J'aime la robe (noir/noire).
8   La rue est (étroit/étroite).
9   Il est (bavard/bavarde).
10 L'eau (chaud/chaude).

To make these adjectives plural you need only add an -s. So describing a noun as 'small' might be spelt petit, petite, petits or petites.

Agreement of adjectives – irregular spelling patterns

Some adjectives do not follow the regular pattern of adding an -e for the feminine and an -s for the plural. There are a few other patterns to learn:

Adjectives ending ...	Change to ...	Examples
-f	-ve	*sportif, neuf, actif* *sportive, neuve, active*
-x	-se	*affreux, heureux* *affreuse, heureuse*
-s	-sse	*bas, gros, gras* *basse, grosse, grasse*
-n	-nne	*bon, ancien* *bonne, ancienne*
-l	-lle	*gentil, traditionnel* *gentille, traditionnelle*
-eau	-elle	*beau, nouveau* *belle, nouvelle*
-er	-ère	*cher, fier, premier* *chère, fière, première*
-c	-che or -que	*sec, public, blanc* *seche, publique, blanche*

A few adjectives ending in -x have their own rules. They simply have to be learnt as they are: *doux* becomes *douce*, *faux* becomes *fausse*, and *vieux* becomes *vieille* (before a masculine noun beginning with a vowel or silent *h*, *vieux* changes to *vieil*). Similarly, *beau* and *nouveau* change to *bel* and *nouvel* when they come before a noun beginning with a vowel or a silent *h*. Some adjectives, like *marron* or *chocolat*, never ever change, and neither do adjectives made up of two words, like *bleu marine* or *bleu foncé*.

The adjectives simply did not agree!

Exercise E

Complete these sentences with the correctly spelt adjective:

1 *Tes soeurs sont (bavard).*
2 *Deux maisons (moderne).*
3 *Elle a une (petit) soeur.*
4 *Cette phrase est (faux).*
5 *La (premier) fois.*
6 *J'ai les yeux (marron).*
7 *Son père est (malade).*
8 *Ses frères sont (petit).*
9 *Mme. Dupont est (vieux).*
10 *La langue (grec).*
11 *Une chemise (blanc).*
12 *J'ai les cheveux (blond).*

Possessive adjectives – my, your, his, her, our, their

Possessive adjectives tell you to whom something belongs: **my** dog, **your** cat, **his** pencil, **her** book, **our** house, **their** brother, and so on. In French, the possessive adjective must 'agree' with the noun – a masculine noun needs a masculine possessive adjective, a feminine noun needs a feminine possessive adjective, and a plural nouns will require a plural possessive adjective. This table shows all the words you will need to learn:

He found it surprisingly easy to relate to possessive pronouns

	my	your (tu)	his/her	our	your (vous)	their
masculine	mon	ton	son	notre	votre	leur
feminine	ma	ta	sa			
plural	mes	tes	ses	nos	vos	leurs

In English, you might say his pen or her pen, depending on the owner. In French, the possessive adjective is decided by the noun – in this case the pen, which is masculine – so *son stylo* means either his pen or her pen.

Feminine nouns that begin with a vowel use the masculine possessive adjective to make it easier to say. So, for example, *mon ami* and *mon amie* (**not** *ma amie*).

 Exercise F

Can you choose the correct possessive adjective?

a   *Mon, ma or mes?*

1 *copain*	4 *frère*	7 *gomme*	10 *maison*
2 *sac*	5 *crayons*	8 *règle*	11 *soeurs*
3 *amis*	6 *baskets*	9 *écharpe*	12 *parents*

b   *Ton, ta or tes?*

1 *vacances*	4 *frères*	7 *livres*	10 *chien*
2 *sac*	5 *crayons*	8 *petite amie*	11 *soeur*
3 *amis*	6 *jupe*	9 *amie*	12 *parents*

c   *Son, sa or ses?*

1 *copains*	4 *père*	7 *calculette*	10 *copine*
2 *parents*	5 *crayon*	8 *règle*	11 *soeur*
3 *amie*	6 *enfants*	9 *chapeau*	12 *pull*

d   *Notre or nos?*

1 *valise*	3 *parents*	5 *professeur*	7 *réservation*
2 *animaux*	4 *vacances*	6 *voyage*	8 *amies*

e   *Votre or vos?*

1 *enfants*	3 *père*	5 *billets*	7 *amis*
2 *parents*	4 *passeport*	6 *clés*	8 *nom*

f   *Leur or leurs?*

1 *enfants*	3 *voiture*	5 *billets*	7 *amis*
2 *argent*	4 *chambre*	6 *clés*	8 *adresse*

Interrogative adjectives – asking 'Which?'

'Which' is an adjective that asks a question about a noun – it is called an 'interrogative adjective'. The French equivalent is the word *'quel'* but the spelling changes to 'agree' with the noun. As in all cases with adjectives, a masculine noun requires a masculine adjective, a feminine noun requires a feminine adjective, and plural nouns require plural adjectives.

You won't know which which is which if you can't spell

Singular		Plural	
masculine	feminine	masculine	feminine
quel	quelle	quels	quelles

Exercise G

Complete these questions with the correct spelling of *quel*:

1 ..... *chemise préfères-tu?*

2 *de* ..... *enfants parles-tu?*

3 ..... *matières fais-tu?*

4 ..... *sports fais-tu?*

5 ..... *crayon veux-tu?*

6 ..... *est l'adresse?*

7 ..... *heure est-il?*

8 ..... *est la date?*

Demonstrative adjectives – this, that, these or those?

Demonstrative adjectives point out a particular noun. In English, 'this', 'that', 'these' or 'those' are used. In French, these words are *ce, cet, cette* and *ces*:

masculine	ce
masculine beginning with a vowel or silent *h*	cet
feminine	cette
plural	ces

Exercise H

Complete these phrases with *ce, cet, cette* or *ces*:

1 ..... *soir.*   5 .... *après-midi.*

2 ..... *fille est jolie.*   6 ..... *homme est mon père.*

3 ..... *film est très intéressant.* 7 ..... *robe est trop chère.*

4 ..... *photos sont jolies.*   8 *Regarde* ..... *arbre.*

Comparative adjectives

These are adjectives used to compare two things – bigger, faster, more intelligent, as quiet, etc. To make such comparisons in French, the word *plus* (more), *aussi* (as) or *moins* (less) is added before the adjective – *Paul est grand. Luc est plus grand. Marie est moins grande.* Note that the adjective has to 'agree' with the noun that it is describing.

If you need the word 'than' – bigger than, smaller than – then you will need the French word 'que'. For example, *Il est plus grand que sa soeur.* You must use the same word 'que' with 'aussi' if you want to say, 'as .... as' – *Il est aussi grand que son père.*

Exercise I

Complete these sentences with (=) *aussi*, (+) *plus* or (-) *moins* and a correctly spelt adjective:

1 *Je suis fort mais mon père est* ..... *(+ fort)*

2 *Il est grand mais elle est* ..... *(+ grand)*

3 *Yves est une grosse tête, Paul est beaucoup* ..... *(- intelligent)*

4 *Thomas est très doué mais Marie est* ..... *(= doué)*

5 *Le CD est cher, mais la cassette est* ..... *(- cher)*

Exercise J

Compare the people in these sentences using the adjective *grand* and the comparative which corresponds to the symbol in brackets:

1 *M. Durand est* ..... *M. Dupont. (+)*   4 *Il est* ..... *moi. (+)*

2 *Mme. Laval est* ..... *sa soeur. (-)*   5 *Elle est* ..... *Paul. (-)*

3 *Ma mère est* ..... *mon père. (=)*   6 *Paul est* ..... *toi. (=)*

If you want to say that someone, or something, is the biggest, the smallest, the fastest, etc, then you simply add the French word for 'the' – *le, la, l'* or *les* – before *plus* or *moins*. In all

Biggest, fastest, strongest, clumsiest

these cases, the adjectives used must 'agree' with the noun, ie *Sarah et Marie sont petites mais Nicole est la plus petite.*

Just as you cannot say, 'more good' in English, so the French words for 'good', 'better' and 'best' do not require the use of *plus*. This table shows the spelling variation:

Singular		Plural		English
masculine	feminine	masculine	feminine	
bon	*bonne*	*bons*	*bonnes*	good
meilleur	*meilleure*	*meilleurs*	*meilleures*	better
le meilleur	*la meilleure*	*les meilleurs*	*les meilleures*	best

 Exercise K

Replace the English word in brackets with its French equivalent:

1 *Mon stylo est.....* (better than) *ton stylo et .....* (less expensive).

2 *Cette montagne est .....* *du monde.* (the highest)

3 *Marie est ma .....* *copine.* (best)

4 *Il est un très .....* (good) *élève mais Paul est .....* *élève.* (the best)

5 *Il joue bien, mais Thomas est .....* (better).

4 Verbs

You have probably been told that verbs are 'doing' words. They say what you are doing, or what someone or something else is doing. This is a useful way of identifying many verbs, but it doesn't always help with verbs that don't actually 'do' very much. 'The cat is on the mat' is a sentence, but which word is the verb? Did you correctly say, 'is'?

Luckily the board pen was not loaded!

 Exercise A

Can you identify the verb in each of these English sentences?

1 I hate homework.
2 She arrived late.
3 The phone was ringing.
4 Cats like milk.
5 This book is great.

6 We are all vegetarians.
7 The cat chased the mouse.
8 Dad says, 'No'.
9 How is your Mum?
10 She's watching the film.

The infinitive

The way a verb appears in the dictionary, without a subject, before it is altered in any way, is called the infinitive. In English, this will almost always start with the word 'to' – to read, to write, to speak, to be, to have, etc.

 Exercise B

Use your dictionary to find out the meanings of these infinitives:

1 *rencontrer*
2 *demander*
3 *conduire*
4 *enseigner*
5 *promener*
6 *reconnaître*
7 *dessiner*
8 *choisir*
9 *savoir*
10 *voir*
11 *boire*
12 *cocher*

French infinitives are grouped according to their spelling. There are three groups: those that end in the letters -er, those that end in -ir and those that end in -re. Here are some examples of each group:

-er	-ir	-re
regarder	finir	vendre
écouter	remplir	répondre
travailler	grossir	attendre
jouer	sentir	descendre
aimer	partir	prendre
manger	dormir	comprendre
parler	sortir	apprendre
habiter	réussir	faire

The vast majority (more than 80%) belong to the -er group, but you will need to know about all three groups.

Verbs that follow a regular pattern are called regular verbs, those that do not follow the regular pattern are called irregular verbs. Most verbs are regular, but since many of the most commonly used verbs are irregular, you will need to be confident in dealing with both.

After a full bag of prunes he was a regular verb again...

The present tense: Regular -er verbs

In English, there are three ways of expressing a verb in the present tense; in French, there is only one. So a single French verb can mean any of three slightly different English expressions. *'Je regarde la télé'* can be translated as 'I am watching the TV', 'I watch the TV', or even, 'I do watch TV'. In simple terms, the present tense is used to say what someone is doing now, what they usually do, what is happening now or what usually happens.

Please Miss, is this -er before
or after George Clooney?

Verbs change their spelling according to their subject (who is doing the verb, see page 30). Regular -er verbs are formed by replacing the letters -er with different endings in accordance with the subject of the verb. So, if the subject of the verb changes, so might the verb ending.

This table outlines the pattern of endings that you will need to learn:

		Subject	**Ending**
Singular	1st person	*Je*	-e
	2nd person	*Tu*	-es
	3rd person	*Il*	-e
		Elle	-e
Plural	1st person	*Nous*	-ons
	2nd person	*Vous*	-ez
	3rd person	*Ils*	-ent
		Elles	-ent

It will help you to memorise the order of the subject pronouns if you understand the meaning of 1st person, 2nd person and 3rd person. Imagine that you are alone in a room and talking about yourself (1st person), then someone comes in and you talk to them (2nd person). A third person enters (3rd person) and you start to talk about them. So, in English, it is: I (1st person), you (2nd person), he or she (3rd person) for one person (singular), and we (1st person), you (2nd person) and they (3rd person) for more than one (plural).

Look how these rules are applied to this example of a regular -er verb:

He watches =

Infinitive	remove -er	choose subject pronoun	add ending
regarder	*regard..*	*Il*	*Il regard**e***

We watch =

Infinitive	remove -er	choose subject pronoun	add ending
regarder	*regard..*	*Nous*	*Nous regard**ons***

They watch =

Infinitive	remove -er	choose subject pronoun	add ending
regarder	*regard..*	*Ils or Elles*	*Ils regard**ent***
			*Elles regard**ent***

 Exercise C

Can you write these bracketed examples of regular -er verbs in their correct present tense form?

1 *Tu (regarder) le match?*

2 *Vous (aimer) le rugby?*

3 *Je (porter) un pull noir.*

4 *Il (arriver) à la gare.*

5 *Tu (travailler) ce soir?*

6 *Elle (danser) très bien.*

7 *Ils (détester) les maths.*

8 *Elles (jouer) au tennis.*

9 *Nous (habiter) en ville.*

10 *Je (parler) deux langues.*

Remember, a different spelling does not necessarily mean a different pronunciation. For most verbs, each spelling variation sounds the same unless it ends in -ons or -ez.

Her teacher had spoiled it all by telling her the ending...

The present tense: Regular *-ir* verbs

There are two different patterns for *-ir* verbs. Some verbs, like *finir*, replace the *-ir* with the endings shown below, whilst others, like *dormir*, also remove the preceding letter in their singular forms before adding a different set of endings:

Subject pronoun	Verbs like *finir*	Verbs like *dormir*
Je	**-is** Je finis	**-s** Je dors
Tu	**-is** Tu finis	**-s** Tu dors
Il/Elle/On	**-it** Il /Elle/On finit	**-t** Il/Elle/On dort
Nous	**-issons** Nous finissons	**-ons** Nous dormons
Vous	**-issez** Vous finissez	**-ez** Vous dormez
Ils/Elles	**-issent** Ils/Elles finissent	**-ent** Ils/Elles dorment

 Exercise D

Can you write the bracketed verbs in their correct present tense form?
1 to 6 follow the pattern of *finir*, 7 to 12 follow the pattern of *dormir*.

1 *Tu (finir)*

2 *Elles (réussir)*

3 *Je (choisir)*

4 *Vous (finir)*

5 *Il (remplir)*

6 *On (grossir)*

7 *Vous (sortir)*

8 *Nous (partir)*

9 *Je (dormir)*

10 *Il (repartir)*

11 *Elles (sentir)*

12 *Tu (partir)*

The present tense: Regular *-re* verbs

For these verbs the *-re* is replaced by the following endings:

Subject pronoun	Ending
Je	-s
Tu	-s
Il/Elle/On	-
Nous	-ons
Vous	-ez
Ils/Elles	-ent

Exercise E

Complete these sentences by changing each infinitive in brackets into the correct present tense form:

1 *Vous ... (descendre) l'escalier.*
2 *Nous ... (attendre) le bus.*
3 *Paul ... (descendre) à la gare.*
4 *On ... (vendre) la voiture.*

5 *Je ... (vendre) mon vélo.*
6 *Ils ... (répondre) en Anglais.*
7 *Tu m'... (attendre)?*
8 *J'... (attendre) une lettre.*

You will notice that the regular endings for *nous, vous, ils/elles,* are always the same, ie *nous -ons, vous -ez, ils/elles -ent.*

The present tense: Reflexive verbs

Verbs that you might say 'you do to yourself' are known as reflexive verbs. In English, these verbs might be expressed by adding the words, 'myself', 'yourself', himself', 'herself', 'themselves', etc. For example, I wash myself, he calls himself, they dress themselves. In French, these verbs always have a reflexive pronoun between the subject and the verb.

Mum...I can dress myself!

These are the reflexive pronouns:

Singular		Plural	
myself	me/m'	ourselves	nous
yourself	te/t'	yourselves	vous
him/herself	se/s'	themselves	se/s'

An apostrophe replaces the final e before a verb commencing with a vowel or a silent h.

These verbs usually have better translations in English than using the word for word equivalent:

- *Je m'appelle* = I call myself = I am called
- *Il se lave* = He washes himself = He gets washed
- *Nous nous levons* = We get ourselves up = We get up

In the dictionary, reflexive verbs will appear with the reflexive pronoun *se* in front of them. Here are some of the more useful reflexive verbs:

se coucher	to go to bed
se lever	to get up
se reveiller	to wake up
se laver	to get washed
s'habiller	to get dressed
se promener	to go for a walk
s'appeler	to be called
se doucher	to have a shower

 Exercise F

Can you fill in the reflexive pronoun and the present tense of the verbs in brackets?

1 *Ils ... (se laver)*   3 *Il ... (se doucher)*   5 *Tu ...(se lever)*

2 *Vous ... (s'habiller)*   4 *Nous ... (se reveiller)*   6 *Je ... (se laver)*

The present tense: Irregular verbs

Irregular verbs do not follow the usual rules. They follow their own patterns. Some of the most useful, and therefore the most used, verbs are irregular. There is no other solution than to learn them by heart. There are three in particular that you should expect to learn thoroughly – *avoir*, *être* and *aller*.

avoir = to have		*être* = to be		*aller* = to go	
J'	ai	Je	suis	Je	vais
Tu	as	Tu	es	Tu	vas
Il/Elle/On	a	Il/Elle/On	est	Il/Elle/On	va
Nous	avons	Nous	sommes	Nous	allons
Vous	avez	Vous	êtes	Vous	allez
Ils/Elles	ont	Ils/Elles	sont	Ils/Elles	vont

The GCSE exam requires you to show that you know how to use 'a range of tenses' and these three verbs are the essential tools for doing just that. Learn them as soon as you can and as well as you can.

 Exercise G

Complete these sentences with the present tense of the verb in brackets:

1 *J' ... (avoir) une soeur.*

2 *Vous ... (aller) à la gare?*

3 *On ... (avoir) un grand jardin.*

4 *Ils ... (être) très fatigués.*

5 *Quel âge ... (avoir)-tu?*

6 *Tu ... (être) anglais?*

7 *Nous ... (avoir) deux lapins.*

8 *Elle ... (aller) à la poste.*

9 *Nous ... (être) arrivés.*

10 *Je ... (aller) en Italie.*

Here are the next most commonly needed irregular verbs that you should commit to memory:

devoir = to have to/owe		faire = to do/make		pouvoir = to be able		vouloir = to want	
Je	dois	Je	fais	Je	peux	Je	veux
Tu	dois	Tu	fais	Tu	peux	Tu	veux
Il/Elle/On	doit	Il/Elle/On	fait	Il/Elle/On	peut	Il/Elle/On	veut
Nous	devons	Nous	faisons	Nouv	pouvons	Nous	voulons
Vous	devez	Vous	faites	Vous	pouvez	Vous	voulez
Ils/Elles	doivent	Ils/Elles	font	Ils/Elles	peuvent	Ils/Elles	veulent

These verbs are most commonly used to ask or answer questions.

Imperatives: Giving orders, telling someone what to do

First decide whether the person/people you are giving orders to should be addressed as 'tu' or 'vous' in French (see Subject pronouns, page 30). In French, an order or instruction is given by using either the 'tu' or the 'vous' form of the present tense without the subject pronoun. For -er verbs the final -s is dropped. Which of these examples do you recognise?

tu form	vous form	tu form	vous form
Ouvre	Ouvrez	Viens	Venez
Regarde	Regardez	Note	Notez
Lis	Lisez	Coche	Cochez
Écoute	Écoutez	Mets	Mettez
Réponds	Répondez	Ecris	Ecrivez
Fais	Faites	Range	Rangez
Tourne	Tournez	Sors	Sortez

Your GCSE exam will contain instructions in French. A list of the exam instructions, 'rubrics', is given in the exam syllabus. Ask your teacher for a copy of this list or begin to make your own from the test exercises that you will do from time to time. The more familiar you are with these instruction words, the less time you will waste in the exam trying to understand the questions.

The past: Perfect or imperfect?

When you want to talk about things in the past, things that have happened or that have been done, you will need to use a past tense. There are two main past tenses in French – the perfect and the imperfect. This table will help you decide which to use:

Perfect	Imperfect
happened only once can say exactly when is now over and completed main action	happened frequently can't say when not sure if it is over background describing the past describing the weather describing feelings or thoughts was/were ... ing saying how things 'used to be' describing a state

 Exercise H

Can you say whether these are examples of the perfect or imperfect tense, and explain why?

1 She was tired.
2 The phone rang.
3 I bought a postcard.
4 We saw a robbery.
5 I wanted to go.
6 They were watching.
7 Yesterday we went to the beach.
8 He went to the beach every day.
9 Paul came home at midnight.
10 We lived in Paris for three years.

It might help to imagine that you are a stage director. All the things that are going on in the background will need the imperfect tense, but all the main action will need the perfect tense. Sometimes you will need both in the same sentence.

Exercise I

Can you identify which is the perfect and which is the imperfect in these sentences?

1 The phone was ringing when I came in.

2 She was watching the television when I left.

3 I wanted to go, but she said, 'No'.

4 She was very tired when she arrived.

5 I discovered that when I was five, I wore red dungarees.

I told you, that was all in the past...

but, was she perfect or imperfect?

The past: Perfect tense

The perfect tense is formed by using the present tense of *avoir* or *être* with a past participle (a past participle is simply a way of saying what the verb looks like in the past). So there are three parts you will need to consider:

subject + auxiliary verb + past participle = perfect tense

Just as an auxiliary nurse helps out the real nurses, an auxiliary verb helps out other verbs. The perfect tense always uses an auxiliary verb. The auxiliary verb will always be either *avoir* or *être*.

The past participle is formed in different ways depending on the verb. Verbs with regular past participles follow this pattern:

	-er **verbs**	*-ir* **verbs**	*-re* **verbs**
take off	-er	-ir	-re
replace with	-é	-i	-u
example	jouer ▶ joué	sortir ▶ sorti	répondre ▶ répondu

Past participles that do not follow this pattern are called irregular. Here are the most commonly used irregular past participles:

Verb	Irregular past participle
avoir	*eu*
boire	*bu*
devoir	*dû*
lire	*lu*
recevoir	*reçu*
voir	*vu*
prendre	*pris*
apprendre	*appris*
comprendre	*compris*
mettre	*mis*
faire	*fait*
dire	*dit*
écrire	*écrit*

Past participles do not change their spelling if the subject is changed so they are quite easy to learn. You need only remember to change the present tense of the auxiliary verb *avoir* or *être*. This is why you should know the verbs *avoir* and *être* very well indeed.

The perfect tense: Is the auxiliary verb *Avoir* or *Être*?

The perfect tense is made up of three parts:

Subject + auxiliary verb (*avoir* or *être*) + past participle

You will have no choice for the subject or the past participle, but you must learn to decide between *avoir* and *être* for the auxiliary verb.

There are a few mind maps and diagrams that will help you to recall verbs that require *être* as their auxiliary verb. Here are two ways to help you:

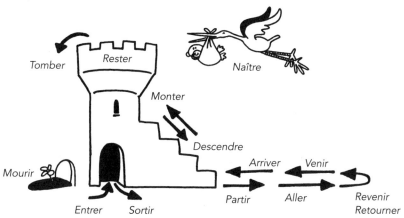

Since neither of these diagrams, however memorable, actually covers all the possible exceptions, you may prefer to rely on the following rather bizarre question:

'If I (verb), would I describe myself as (past participle)?'

If you answer 'Yes' to the above question, then you will need to use *être* as the auxiliary verb. On the other hand, if the answer is 'No', then you will need to use *avoir*. Here are a few examples:

- 'If I eat, would I describe myself as eaten?' No   *J'ai mangé*
- 'If I go, would I describe myself as gone?' Yes   *Je suis allé*
- 'If I buy, would I describe myself as bought?' No *J'ai acheté*
- 'If I leave, would I describe myself as left?' Yes   *Je suis parti*

Since whenever you answer 'Yes', the past participle is being used to describe someone or something, you must apply the rules of agreement just as you would for any 'describing word' or adjective (see page 40).

 ### Exercise J

Can you complete these sentences by adding the correct auxiliary verb in its present tense?

1 *J' ... mangé une pomme.*   5 *Elle ... arrivée hier.*

2 *Nous ... regardé le match.*   6 *Tu ... vu Hélène?*

3 *Il ... parti à 7 heures.*   7 *On ... beaucoup travaillé.*

4 *Sam et Paul ... rentrés tard.* 8 *Elles ... joué au tennis.*

 ### Exercise K

Can you complete these sentences by adding the past participle and the correct auxiliary verb in its present tense?

1 *Elle ... (descendre) en ville.*   5 *Vous ... (écouter) la radio?*

2 *Tu ... (entendre) ce bruit?*   6 *On ... (manger) au café.*

3 *Il ... (avoir) un accident.*   7 *Nous ... (faire) du vélo.*

4 *Paul ... (prendre) le bus.*   8 *J' ... (lire) des BD.*

The perfect tense: Reflexive verbs

All reflexive verbs (see page 54) use *être* to form the perfect tense. The auxiliary verb (*être*) and the past participle stay together and the reflexive pronoun comes immediately after the subject. Look at these examples: *Il s'est couché, elle s'est lavée, ils se sont levés.*

You will notice that since the auxiliary *être* has been used, the past participles must 'agree' (see page 42).

 ### Exercise L

Can you write these sentences in the perfect tense by adding the correct reflexive pronoun and the auxiliary *être* in its present tense?

1 *Elle ... (se coucher) tard.*
2 *Vous ... (se réveiller) à quelle heure?*
3 *Il ... (s'habiller) dans sa chambre.*
4 *Sam et Paul ... (se disputer).*
5 *Nous ... (se lever).*
6 *Tu ... (se laver)?*
7 *On ... (s'approcher).*
8 *Elles ... (s'ennuyer).*

The past: The imperfect tense

To know when to use the imperfect tense you will need to refer back to the beginning of this section. However, in short, it is used to describe the past, what someone or something 'was doing', how things 'used to' be, how someone felt about it, or to describe the weather.

I 'USED TO' ENJOY FRENCH...

Yet another imperfect example...

To form the imperfect tense, you must:

- start with the '*nous*' form of the present tense.
- now ignore the word '*nous*' and take off *-ons*.
- what is left is the 'stem' to which the endings should be added, ie *jou-, mange-, fais-, finiss-, dorm-, répond-*, etc.
- The exception to this rule is the verb *être* whose stem is *ét-*.

All verbs use the same
endings to form the imperfect:

Subject pronoun	Ending
Je	*-ais*
Tu	*-ais*
Il/Elle/On	*-ait*
Nous	*-ions*
Vous	*-iez*
Ils/Elles	*-aient*

 Exercise M

Can you complete these sentences by adding the imperfect of the
verbs in brackets?

1 *Il ... (jouer) au foot.*

2 *Tu ... (écouter) la musique?*

3 *Elles ... (être) fatiguées.*

4 *Mes parents ... (vouloir) venir.*

5 *Quand j' ... (avoir) 2 ans.*

6 *Nous ... (attendre) le bus.*

7 *Paul ...(regarder) la télé.*

8 *C' ... (être) chouette!*

9 *On ... (faire) du cheval.*

10 *Vous ... (lire) le journal?*

The past: Perfect or Imperfect? Which one do I use?

Study the use of the perfect and the imperfect as outlined in this
section, then look at this extract from an imaginary day out.

 Exercise N

Can you correctly identify which past tense to use?

Hier, (je suis allé/j'allais) en ville. (Je suis allé/J'allais) parce que (j'ai
voulu/je voulais) acheter un cadeau pour mon frère. C'(a été/était) son
anniversaire. (Il a fait beau/Il faisait beau) et (j'ai eu/j'avais) envie d'y
aller à pied, mais c'est assez loin et je suis paresseux donc (j'ai pris/je
prenais) le bus et (je suis descendu/je descendais) au centre
commercial. (J'ai fait/Je faisais) les magasins quand (j'ai vu/je voyais)
exactement ce que (j'ai cherché/je cherchais). (Je suis entré/J'entrais)
dans le magasin et (je l'ai acheté/je l'achetais). C' (a été/était) une
casquette avec la phrase, "Mon frère est parfait!"

5 The future

Whenever you want to talk about the future, there are two ways of doing this, just as there are in English. You can say that something 'is going' to happen or that something 'will' happen. The first of these, sometimes called the simple future, needs only the verb *aller* in its present tense form followed by an infinitive. The second, sometimes called the definite future, requires the future tense.

I see tall... dark... and very simple

The future: *Aller* + infinitive (simple future)

You will need to know the present tense of the verb *aller* (see page 56), and you will need to understand what is meant by the infinitive (see page 49). If you already know both of these, then the rest is easy. You will need:

The present tense of *aller* + the infinitive

Here are a few examples: *Je vais regarder la télé, il va écouter la musique, nous allons arriver à 7 heures, tu vas venir?, on va prendre le train.*

 Exercise A

Can you say what these people are going to do by using *aller* plus the infinitive?

1 *Je ... (faire) mes devoirs.*
2 *Tu ... (rester) en Angleterre.*
3 *Vous ... (jouer) au basket?*
4 *Marie ... (prendre) le bus.*
5 *Les enfants ... (dormir).*
6 *Ils ... (écouter) les infos.*
7 *Mon père ... (travailler).*
8 *Paul et Sam ... (sortir).*
9 *Nous ... (regarder) le film.*
10 *On ... (gagner) le match.*

The future tense: Regular verbs

The future tense in French is used to say what someone 'will' do, or what 'will' happen. It is quite easy to learn. To form the future tense you simply add a set of endings to the infinitive (for -re verbs you will also need to take off the last -e). Look at these endings... do they look familiar?

Subject pronoun	Ending
Je	-ai
Tu	-as
Il/Elle/On	-a
Nous	-ons
Vous	-ez
Ils/Elles	-ont

Miss had predicted his future detention with uncanny accuracy

Apart from the 'nous' and the 'vous' endings, the endings are the present tense of the verb *avoir* and, since the *nous* and *vous* endings are the same as the present tense endings that you would expect for all verbs, there is nothing new to learn. This set of endings can be applied to all regular verbs in their future tense.

 Exercise B

Can you say what these people 'will' do by putting the verbs in brackets into the future tense?

1 *Tu* .... *(arriver) à 7 heures.*
2 *Paul* .... *(finir) bientôt.*
3 *Maman* .... *(acheter) une moto.*
4 *Ils* .... *(manger) après le film.*
5 *J'y* .... *(retourner) demain.*
6 *Nous* .... *(sortir) ensemble.*

The future tense: Irregular verbs

Some of the most common verbs are irregular in the future tense, but they still have the same endings as all the others. This means that the stem is not the infinitive but the endings remain the same. The only way to deal with these irregular verbs is to learn them as vocabulary. Since they are so common, you will get plenty of opportunities to practise.

Infinitive	Stem	Example
avoir	**aur-**	J'aurai
être	**ser-**	Tu seras
aller	**ir-**	Il ira
devoir	**devr-**	Elle devra
faire	**fer-**	On fera
pouvoir	**pourr-**	Nous pourrons
savoir	**saur-**	Vous saurez
venir	**viendr-**	Ils viendront
voir	**verr-**	Elles verront
vouloir	**voudr-**	Je voudrai

 Exercise C

Can you say what the future holds for these people?

1 J' .... (avoir) une fête.

2 Ils .... (pouvoir) partir.

3 Nous .... (savoir) demain.

4 Paul .... (aller) au stade.

5 Anne et Chloé .... (être) sages.

6 Tu .... (faire) un voyage.

7 Vous .... (voir) la différence.

8 Il .... (être) de retour.

9 Elle .... (faire) du vélo.

10 Vous .... (devoir) y aller.

6 The conditional

If you want to say what 'would' or 'could' happen, rather than what 'will', you need to use the conditional. If you already know the future tense (see page 65), and you are familiar with the imperfect endings (see page 63), then the conditional is very easy indeed.

To form the conditional:

- the same stem is used as in the future tense
- the endings added are exactly the same as the imperfect endings: *-ais, -ais, -ait, -ions, -iez, -aient.*

 Exercise A

Complete these sentences using the conditional of the verb in brackets:

1 *S'il pleut, je (rester) à la maison.*
2 *Il (être) content de te voir.*
3 *Elles (faire) leurs devoirs à la table.*
4 *Je (vouloir) du pain.*
5 *Tu (pouvoir) venir.*
6 *On (prendre) le bus.*

7 Negatives

The negative is used when you want to say 'no' or 'not'. In English, the words don't, can't, hasn't or haven't are often used to make a negative statement. For example, I know, I don't know; I swim, I can't swim; I have a cat, I haven't got a cat.

Which part of Ne…pas did you not understand?

To form the negative in French, you will need to add two little words – *ne* is placed in front of the verb and *pas* is placed after it: *je ne sais pas, il ne joue pas, elle n'a pas, tu n'habites pas*, etc.

You will notice that the *ne* becomes *n'* before a verb that starts with a vowel or a silent *h*.

 ## Exercise A

Can you add *ne* and *pas* to these sentences so that nobody is doing anything?

1 *Elle regarde la télé.*
2 *Elles écoutent la radio.*
3 *Nous allons au cinéma.*
4 *Ils habitent à Paris.*
5 *Je joue au golf.*
6 *On mange des frites.*
7 *Vous travaillez.*
8 *Marie-Ange vient.*

Negatives and the perfect tense

To form the negative in the perfect tense, you will need to put the *ne* and the *pas* around the auxiliary verb – *avoir* or *être* – rather than around the main verb. For example, *je n'ai pas mangé, il n'est pas allé, tu n'as pas regardé*, etc.

So, how come we ain't not never done nothing like this in English?

 ## Exercise B

Can you correctly place *ne* and *pas* into these perfect tense phrases to turn them into negative statements?

1 *Je suis allé.*
2 *Il est resté à la maison.*
3 *Vous avez téléphoné.*
4 *Marie et Claire sont arrivées.*
5 *Nous avons joué au tennis.*
6 *Tu es parti sans elle.*
7 *Paul a fait du vélo.*
8 *Elles ont travaillé.*

Negatives: Other negative expressions

There are a few other words that can be used instead of *pas* in negative expressions. The words are usually placed in the same positions as *pas*, but each one has a different meaning.

So, a simple phrase like, *je mange*, might become:

• *Je ne mange pas*	I do not eat
• *Je ne mange plus*	I do not eat anymore
• *Je ne mange rien*	I eat nothing
• *Je ne mange jamais*	I never eat
• *Je ne mange personne*	I eat no-one
• *Je ne mange ni ... ni ...*	I eat neither ... nor ...
• *Je ne mange que ...*	I only eat ...

 ### Exercise C

Can you place the right negative expression into these sentences?

1 *Je suis allé.* (never)

2 *Il attend.* (no-one)

3 *Tu as gagné.* (nothing)

4 *Elles ont un franc.* (only)

5 *Nous jouons au tennis.* (no longer)

6 *Tu bois du café et du thé.* (neither)

7 *Paul a fait du vélo.* (only)

8 *Ils sont arrivés.* (never)

8 Adverbs

An adverb is a word that describes a verb, or tells you more about it. Most adverbs describe how something is or was done, but some add information about where, when and to what extent: 'far', 'soon' and 'very' are all adverbs.

In English, adverbs are usually made by adding -ly to an adjective: quickly, slowly, happily, normally, etc. In French, the normal rule is to add *-ment* to the feminine form of the adjective: *lentement, doucement, heureusement, sérieusement*, etc. There are, of course, exceptions to this rule. Adjectives that end in *i* or *u* form their adverb from the masculine: *vraiment, poliment, absolument*, etc and a few adjectives need an accent on the *-e* before *-ment* when they become adverbs: *profondément, énormément, précisément*, etc.

Some commonly occuring adverbs look very different from their corresponding adjective and will need to be learned:

Adjective		Adverb	
bon	good	*bien*	well
mauvais	bad	*mal*	badly
petit	small	*peu*	little
meilleur	better	*mieux*	better
rapide	quick	*vite*	quickly

There are even some adverbs without a corresponding adjective:

bientôt	soon	*près*	near
souvent	often	*assez*	enough/quite
soudain	suddenly	*beaucoup*	a lot
demain	tomorrow	*très*	very
loin	far	*quelquefois*	sometimes

Exercise A

Insert the adverb that corresponds to the adjective shown:

1 *Vous parlez ... (rapide).*
2 *Elle chante ... (doux).*
3 *Non. (Absolu) ... pas!*
4 *Tu joues ... (bon).*
5 *(Normal) ... , on finit à 4h.*
6 *J'ai ... (mauvais) dormit.*

How do you do that?

9 Prepositions

Prepositions are words placed before nouns and pronouns that give information about where, when, how, for whom, or to whom. The two most frequently used prepositions are the little French words *à* and *de*.

Prepositions: *à*

À is used either on its own or combined with the definite article (*le, la, l', les*). The spelling depends on the combination:

$$à + le \ = \ au$$
$$à + la \ = \ à \ la$$
$$à + l' \ = \ à \ l'$$
$$à + les \ = \ aux$$

You will need to know when to use *à* on its own and when to combine it with the definite article. It is used on its own in expressions of time, possession, prices, distances and before the name of all towns and cities (unless they have the word *Le* as part of their name!). It is used with the definite article when referring to places around town, masculine countries (feminine ones use the preposition *en*), and for flavours and sorts of sandwiches.

 Exercise A

Use *à* or *à* plus the definite article to complete these sentences:

1 *Je vais ... plage*   4 *Je vais ... collège*   7 *Il va ... stade*
2 *Elle va ... Canada*   5 *On va ... Paris*   8 *Il va ... Le Mans*
3 *Tu finis ... midi*   6 *Une glace ... fraise*   9 *Un timbre ... 5F*

Prepositions: *De*

De is also used either on its own or with the definite article (*le, la, l', les*). Its spelling sometimes changes depending on the combination, so you will need to know when to use which. As a simple guide, it will help to know that *de* is used on its own to mean of, from (a town) or with, and it will become *d'* before a vowel or a silent *h*.

At other times, it is used with the definite article and its spelling may change:

de + le = du
de + la = de la
de + l' = de l'
de + les = des

I think he's prepositioning us...

 Exercise B

Use *de* or *de* plus the definite article to complete these sentences:

1 *Je voudrais ... pain.*
2 *Un paquet ... chips.*
3 *Il vient ... Paris.*
4 *Près ... Londres.*
5 *J'ai ... amis en France.*

6 *Je voudrais ... limonade.*
7 *Un kilo ... oranges.*
8 *En face ... gare.*
9 *Beaucoup ... livres.*
10 *La chambre ... mes parents.*

Prepositions: Saying where or when

Other prepositions are used to say where something is or when something happens. Here are the most useful prepositions in each case:

Saying where something is		Saying when something happens	
chez	at (house/shop)	*à*	at
dans	in	*après*	after
derrière	behind	*avant*	before
devant	in front of	*depuis*	for/since
en	in	*en*	in
entre	between	*pendant*	during
sous	under	*pour*	for
sur	on	*vers*	about

10 Numbers

You will need to know your numbers well for the GCSE exam and if you are hoping to spend some time in France.

0	*zéro*	10	*dix*	20	*vingt*
1	*un/une*	11	*onze*	21	*vingt et un*
2	*deux*	12	*douze*	22	*vingt-deux*
3	*trois*	13	*treize*	30	*trente*
4	*quatre*	14	*quatorze*	40	*quarante*
5	*cinq*	15	*quinze*	50	*cinquante*
6	*six*	16	*seize*	60	*soixante*
7	*sept*	17	*dix-sept*	70 71	*soixante-dix* *soixante-onze*, etc.
8	*huit*	18	*dix-huit*	80 81	*quatre-vingts* *quatre-vingt-un*, etc.
9	*neuf*	19	*dix-neuf*	90 91	*quatre-vingt-dix* *quatre-vingt-onze*, etc.

Big numbers and small numbers

1/2	*un demi (la moitié)*	100	*cent*
1/3	*un tiers*	101	*cent un*
2/3	*deux tiers*	200	*deux cents*
1/4	*un quart*	210	*deux cent dix*
3/4	*trois quarts*	300	*trois cents*
decimal point	use comma (*virgule*)	1000	*mille*
ie 0.4	ie 0,4	2000	*deux mille*
		1310	*mille trois cent dix*
		1 000 000	*un million*
		1 000 000 000	*un milliard*

Ordinal numbers

1st *première (1er)* 4th *quatrième*
2nd *deuxième* 5th *cinquième*, etc
3rd *troisième*

11 Date and time

Telling the time

This diagram is all you need to recall to help you tell the time with confidence in French:

Past the hour

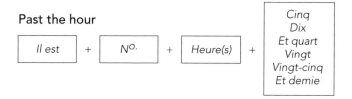

$$\boxed{Il\ est} + \boxed{N^o.} + \boxed{Heure(s)} + \boxed{\begin{array}{l}Cinq \\ Dix \\ Et\ quart \\ Vingt \\ Vingt\text{-}cinq \\ Et\ demie\end{array}}$$

To the hour

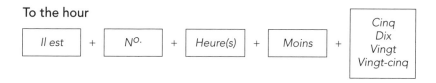

$$\boxed{Il\ est} + \boxed{N^o.} + \boxed{Heure(s)} + \boxed{Moins} + \boxed{\begin{array}{l}Cinq \\ Dix \\ Vingt \\ Vingt\text{-}cinq\end{array}}$$

Days, months and dates

Days of the week are usually written without capital letters:

> *lundi, mardi, mercredi, jeudi, vendredi, samedi, dimanche*

= *Monday, Tuesday, Wednesday, Thursday, Friday, Saturday, Sunday*

Months of the year are usually written without capital letters:

> *janvier, février, mars, avril, mai, juin, juillet, août, septembre, octobre, novembre, décembre*

= *January, February, March, April, May, June, July, August, September, October, November, December*

Date:

> *mardi, le 5 avril* or *le mardi 5 avril*

Periods of time

> *Un mois, deux mois, tous les mois, chaque mois*

= *One month, two months, every month, each and every month*

> *Un an, une année, toute l'année, tous les ans*

= *One year, the whole year, all year, every year*

Seasons

> *l'hiver, en hiver, le printemps, au printemps,*
> *l'été, en été, l'automne, en automne*

= *winter, in winter, spring, in spring,*
  summer, in summer, autumn, in autumn.

5 Language tasks by topic

GCSE examination topics vary slightly depending on the chosen syllabus, but this checklist (see overpage) will help you monitor your progress within the topics of the National Curriculum Areas of Experience. The boxes allow you to tick when you have learned each one. Later, you can also tick when you have revised it.

Area of Experience A: Everyday activities

A1: Language of the classroom

	Learned	Revised
• Understand classroom instructions	☐	☐
• Make simple classroom requests	☐	☐
• Say I don't know, don't understand or ask someone to repeat something	☐	☐
• Ask for the spelling out of words	☐	☐
• Ask what things are called in English or French	☐	☐
• Ask what words or phrases mean	☐	☐
• Ask someone to explain a word	☐	☐

A2: School

	Learned	Revised
• Ask for/give information about school subjects and facilities	☐	☐
• Express simple opinions about school, giving reasons	☐	☐
• Ask for and give details about school routine: when school begins and ends, how many lessons there are, how long they last, break- and lunch-times, homework	☐	☐
• Ask for and give details of extra-curricular activities	☐	☐
• Say how long I have been learning French or other language	☐	☐
• Discuss school timetables, terms and holidays	☐	☐
• Discuss school subjects, rules, uniform	☐	☐
• Understand information about different types of school	☐	☐

A3: Home life

- Say what jobs I do around the house ☐ ☐
- Describe the house/flat I live in and its location ☐ ☐
- Find out about and give simple details of rooms, garage, garden: location, colour, size, contents ☐ ☐
- Ask about taking a bath or shower ☐ ☐
- Say I need/ask others if they need soap/toothpaste/towel ☐ ☐
- Ask where rooms are in a house ☐ ☐
- State, and ask others, at what time they have meals ☐ ☐
- Discuss and express opinions about typical meals, meal times and eating habits ☐ ☐
- Offer and ask for help to do something around the house ☐ ☐
- Discuss to what extent members of the family help at home ☐ ☐
- Say whether I have a room of my own or share a room ☐ ☐

A4: Media

- Understand simple information about TV programmes, radio, music, performers ☐ ☐
- Ask permission to use the telephone, the radio or watch TV ☐ ☐
- State which programmes or films I have seen recently, or what music I have heard: when, where ☐ ☐
- Express simple opinions about newspapers, magazines, TV programmes, radio, music, performers ☐ ☐
- Understand and narrate plots of TV programmes, news items or books ☐ ☐
- Ask for and give opinions about newspapers, magazines, programmes, radio, music, performers ☐ ☐

A5: Health and fitness

- Say how I feel (well, ill, better, cold, hot, hungry, thirsty, tired) and ask others how they feel ☐ ☐
- Say whether I have a pain or other discomfort ☐ ☐
- Call for help ☐ ☐
- Make arrangements to consult a doctor, dentist or chemist ☐ ☐
- Ask and answer questions about treatment for common ailments at a doctor's, dentist's or chemist's ☐ ☐
- Discuss healthy and unhealthy lifestyles ☐ ☐

A6: Food

- Express simple opinions about food ☐ ☐
- Ask for food and table items ☐ ☐
- Attract waiter's/waitress' attention and ask for the bill ☐ ☐
- Order drinks, snacks or simple meals ☐ ☐
- Ask about the availability of food and drink ☐ ☐
- Ask for an explanation of something on the menu ☐ ☐
- Ask where the toilet or telephone is ☐ ☐
- Accept/decline offers of food or drink, giving reasons ☐ ☐
- Express appreciation and pay compliments ☐ ☐
- Ask others if they need food or table items ☐ ☐
- Ask for a little, a lot, more – say I have enough ☐ ☐
- Ask for a table – state number of people ☐ ☐
- State preference for seating: inside, terrace, near window ☐ ☐
- Make a complaint, giving reasons ☐ ☐
- Ask about service charges ☐ ☐

Area of Experience B: Personal and social life

B1: Self, family and friends

- Ask for and give information about self, family, friends and pets: name, age and birthday, nationality, likes and dislikes (with regard to people and other topics in the syllabus), physical appearance, character ☐ ☐
- Spell/understand the spelling of names/streets/towns ☐ ☐
- State/understand others stating gender, marital status ☐ ☐
- Describe character and personality ☐ ☐
- Express feelings about others ☐ ☐

B2: Free time, holidays and special occasions

- Give/seek/understand information about hobbies/ interests ☐ ☐
- Describe recent holiday or leisure activities ☐ ☐
- Ask for and give information about times and prices at swimming pools, stadiums, sports centres, leisure facilities ☐ ☐
- Buy tickets for sporting activities ☐ ☐
- Say how much pocket money I get and how I spend it ☐ ☐

- Say whether I am a member of any clubs and
  what I do there ☐ ☐
- Discuss my holiday, weekend and evening activities
  and those of others ☐ ☐
- Discuss preferences and alternatives for going out ☐ ☐

B3: Personal and social life
- Greet someone and respond to greetings,
  ask how they are ☐ ☐
- Welcome and receive a visitor ☐ ☐
- Thank someone for hospitality ☐ ☐
- Ask permission to do things ☐ ☐
- Apologise appropriately ☐ ☐
- Discuss problems appropriate to my age, experience
  and interests ☐ ☐

B4: Arranging a meeting or activity
- Make simple suggestions for going out, and
  invite someone/somwhere ☐ ☐
- Accept or decline an invitiation and express pleasure ☐ ☐
- Ask about, suggest or confirm a time and place to meet ☐ ☐
- Find out whether a particular facility/entertainment is
  available and discuss options ☐ ☐

B5: Leisure and entertainment
- Ask what is on at the cinema, or what sort of
  concert there is ☐ ☐
- Find out the cost of seats and buy tickets for
  cinema or concert ☐ ☐
- Find out or state the start or finishing time of a
  film/concert ☐ ☐
- Ask for or express an opinion about a film/concert ☐ ☐
- Understand and narrate the main features of a film or play ☐ ☐

Area of Experience C: The world around us

C1: Home town, local environment and customs

- Give a simple description of, and express simple opinions about, my home town, neighbourhood and region: location, character, amenities, features of interest ☐ ☐
- Say how I travel into town: means of transport, duration of journey ☐ ☐
- Give simple information, and express simple opinions about important festivals ☐ ☐
- Understand a description of a town or region ☐ ☐
- Understand and make comparisons between home country and French-speaking country/community: towns, regions, climate and geographical features ☐ ☐
- Express and explain opinions about where I live ☐ ☐
- Give weather predictions and understand simple forecasts ☐ ☐

C2: Finding the way

- Attract the attention of a passer-by and ask for directions ☐ ☐
- Ask/state where a place is ☐ ☐
- State if there is a place nearby or enquire if it is near/far ☐ ☐

C3: Shopping

- Ask where particular shops/supermarkets are ☐ ☐
- Ask about and understand opening/closing times ☐ ☐
- Ask for items, giving simple description: colour, size, for whom ☐ ☐
- Express quantity required: weight, volume, container ☐ ☐
- Ask and understand about non-availability ☐ ☐
- Understand/reply to the question, "Is that all?" ☐ ☐
- Express simple opinions about clothes ☐ ☐
- Find particular goods and departments within a store ☐ ☐
- Discuss shopping habits, facilities and preferences ☐ ☐
- Say I will/will not buy something, giving the reason ☐ ☐
- Ask for a refund or replacement ☐ ☐
- Understand information about discounts, special offers, reductions and sales ☐ ☐

C4: Public services

- Ask where a post office, Tabac or letter-box is ☐ ☐
- Say I would like to send a letter/postcard/parcel and ask the cost ☐ ☐
- Ask for stamps ☐ ☐
- Ask whether there is a telephone nearby ☐ ☐
- Exchange money or traveller's cheques ☐ ☐
- Ask for coins of a particular denomination ☐ ☐
- Report a loss or theft, saying what has been lost, when and where and giving a description of the item lost: what it is made of, size, shape, colour, make, contents ☐ ☐

C5: Getting around

- Understand simple signs and notices ☐ ☐
- Ask if there is a bus/train/coach to a particular place ☐ ☐
- Ask about location of facilities/bus stop/toilets/platform ☐ ☐
- Buy tickets or carnet of tickets specifying details: destination, single/return, class, day of travel ☐ ☐
- Ask for information about times of departure and arrival ☐ ☐
- Ask for or give directions/information about public transport ☐ ☐
- Buy fuel and obtain services at a service station ☐ ☐
- Report basic details of an accident or motor breakdown ☐ ☐

Area of Experience D: The world of work

D1: Further education and training

- Understand, ask for and give information about future plans ☐ ☐
- Discuss and understand others describing education/ training and future plans ☐ ☐

D2: Careers and employment

- Give information about my travel to place of work: times, means of transport, duration of journey ☐ ☐
- Understand and say that someone is out of work ☐ ☐
- Ask/understand details of jobs or work experience ☐ ☐
- State occupation of self, family and others ☐ ☐
- Understand the names of occupations commonly encountered ☐ ☐
- Understand/ask for/give reasons for choice of study training ☐ ☐
- Express hopes for future/plans for after formal education ☐ ☐
- Understand/give opinions about different jobs ☐ ☐
- Enquire about the availability of suitable work ☐ ☐
- Discuss the advantages/disadvantages of different jobs ☐ ☐

D3: Advertising and publicity

- Understand publicity about leisure activities or public events ☐ ☐
- Understand/give an opinion about particular advertisements ☐ ☐

D4: Communication

- Ask for and give telephone number ☐ ☐
- Answer telephone call, stating name ☐ ☐
- Make telephone call and ask to speak to someone ☐ ☐
- Take/leave a simple message: name, telephone number, time to call back ☐ ☐
- Obtain coins or phone card ☐ ☐

Area of Experience E: The international world

E1: Life in other countries/communities

- Understand money, including written and printed prices ☐ ☐
- Discuss typical foods and how to prepare them ☐ ☐
- Discuss important social conventions: forms of address, eating habits ☐ ☐

E2: Tourism

- Talk and enquire about holidays: where and with whom, for how long, what I do ☐ ☐
- Describe previous holiday: where I went, with whom, for how long, where I stayed, weather, what I saw and did, what my general impressions were ☐ ☐
- Ask for/give details of excursions: cost, time, destination ☐ ☐
- Request tourist publicity ☐ ☐

E3: Accommodation

- Ask whether rooms are available ☐ ☐
- State when I require a room and for how long ☐ ☐
- Say what sort of room I require, accept or reject ☐ ☐
- Ask the cost: per person, per night, per room ☐ ☐
- Ask where facilities are: restaurant, toilet, shower/bathroom, garage ☐ ☐
- Ask for details of meal times ☐ ☐
- Arrange accommodation at hotels, youth hostels and campsites for myself and for others ☐ ☐
- Seek/understand information about rules and regulations ☐ ☐

E4: The wider world

- Understand names of countries and nationalities commonly encountered ☐ ☐
- Discuss environmental issues of personal interest ☐ ☐
- Understand information and opinions about global issues ☐ ☐
- Discuss any part of France (or French-speaking country) I know about and describe it in simple terms: its history, geography, current and future developments ☐ ☐

Short Course topics

If you are doing a GCSE Short Course in French, then you need only study two topics. Your teachers will choose from those listed in the National Curriculum Areas of Experience.

6 Vocabulary by topic

Your teacher might produce vocabulary lists from those provided in the syllabus. However, this vocabulary list by GCSE topic should get you started on creating your own. It does **not** have all the words you might need in it – if it did, it would be called a dictionary and you should already have one of those!

To give you an indication of the range of vocabulary you will need to know, some useful words and expressions appear in French with their English meanings. Space has been allowed for you to list additional vocabulary you might need or find useful.

Things were going in but nothing seemed to stick…

Area of Experience A: Everyday activities

 Language of the classroom

apprendre	to learn	*le mot*	word
le cahier	exercise book	*un ordinateur*	computer
c'est-à-dire	that means	*oublier*	to forget
comment	how (pardon?)	*parler*	to speak
comprendre	to understand	*penser*	to think
copain/copine	friend	*je peux...?*	may I...?
le cours	lesson	*poser une question*	to ask a question
le crayon	pencil	*le/la prof(esseur)*	teacher
désolé(e)	sorry	*la récréation*	break
les devoirs	homework	*répéter*	to repeat
écouter	to listen (to)	*répondre*	to reply
écrire	to write	*savoir*	to know (fact)
épeler	to spell	*le stylo*	pen
étudiant(e)	student	*le tableau*	black/whiteboard
faux/fausse	false	*très*	very
la langue	tongue, language	*trop*	too much
lentement	slowly	*vite*	quickly
lire	to read	*le vocabulaire*	vocabulary
le livre	book	*vrai*	true

....

....

....

....

....

....

....

....

School

d'abord	first of all	*facile*	easy
l'allemand	German	*la gomme*	rubber
après	after	*hier*	yesterday
cet après midi	this afternoon	*l'histoire-géo*	humanities
aujourd'hui	today	*l'informatique*	ICT
en avance	in advance, early	*jouer*	to play
la bibliothèque	library	*loin*	far
la cantine	canteen	*la matière*	subject
le collège	secondary school	*les maths*	maths
la cour	playground	*ce matin*	this morning
demain	tomorrow	*moyenne*	average
dessiner	to draw	*préférer*	to prefer
difficile	difficult	*la règle*	rule, ruler
durer	to last (time)	*en retard*	late
ennuyeux/euse	boring	*la salle*	room
ensuite	next, after	*les sciences*	science
l'espagnol	Spanish	*sévère*	strict
être fort(e) en	to be good at	*les travaux manuels*	CDT crafts
étudier	to study	*les vacances*	holidays

....

....

....

....

....

....

....

....

Home life: Describing the house

un appartement	flat		*louer*	to rent
en bas	downstairs		*la maison*	house/home
le bâtiment	building		*les meubles*	furniture
beau/belle	beautiful		*moderne*	modern
en bois	of wood		*nettoyer*	to clean
le bruit	noise		*neuf/neuve*	new
la clé	key		*petit(e)*	small
chez	at the home of		*pratique*	practical
déménager	to move house		*près de*	near
la ferme	farm		*la rez-de-chaussée*	ground floor
grand(e)	large		*tranquille*	calm, quiet
en haut	upstairs		*typique*	typical
une HLM	council flat		*à vendre*	for sale
un immeuble	block of flats		*vieux/vieille*	old

....

....

....

....

 ## Home life: Rooms and furniture

les allumettes	matches		*la cave*	cellar
un arbre	tree		*la chaise*	chair
une armoire	wardrobe		*la chambre*	bedroom
un ascenceur	lift		*l'eau chaude*	hot water
un aspirateur	vacuum cleaner		*une commode*	drawers
une assiette	plate		*le couloir*	corridor
la baignoire	bath		*le couteau*	knife
le balcon	balcony		*la cuisine*	kitchen
le bol	bowl		*le dentifrice*	toothpaste
le bricolage	DIY		*la douche*	shower

un escalier	staircase		*un placard*	cupboard
un étage	floor, storey		*plusieurs*	several
une étagère	shelf		*la porte*	door
faire la vaisselle	to wash-up		*la poubelle*	rubbish bin
le fauteuil	armchair		*la prise*	plug (electric)
la fenêtre	window		*le rasoir*	razor
fermer	to close		*le réveil*	alarm clock
la fleur	flower		*les rideaux*	curtains
la fourchette	fork		*les lits superposés*	bunk beds
le frigo	fridge		*un tiroir*	drawer
le garage	garage		*le lave-vaisselle*	dishwasher
le jardinage	gardening		*le robinet*	tap
le jardin	garden		*la salle de bain(s)*	bathroom
la lampe	lamp		*la salle à manger*	dining room
le magnétoscope	VCR		*la salle de séjour*	living room
la moquette	carpet		*le salon*	lounge
le mur	wall		*le savon*	soap
ouvrir	to open		*la serviette*	towel
le parking	car park		*le shampooing*	shampoo
partager	to share		*le sous-sol*	basement
la pièce	room		*les toilettes*	toilets

Home life: Daily routine

A quelle heure?	At what time?	*se laver*	to wash
aller chercher	to go and get	*se lever*	to get up
aller voir	to go and see	*manger*	to eat
s'amuser	to have fun	*s'occuper de*	to take care of
avoir besoin de	to be in need of	*le petit-déjeuner*	breakfast
boire	to drink	*Peux-tu ...?*	Can you ...?
se coucher	to go to bed	*passer l'aspirateur*	to hoover
débarasser	to clear (away)	*prendre un bain*	to take a bath
le déjeuner	lunch	*prêter*	to lend
le dîner	supper	*se promener*	to go for a walk
dormir	to sleep	*ranger*	to tidy (away)
s'endormir	to fall asleep	*se raser*	to shave
faire les courses	do the shopping	*regarder*	to watch
faire la cuisine	do the cooking	*rentrer*	to return home
faire le lit	to make the bed	*un repas*	a meal
faire le ménage	do the housework	*se reposer*	to rest
garder les enfants	to look after kids	*sortir*	to go out
le goûter	snack	*travailler*	to work
Je m'en vais	I'm going	*utiliser*	to use
Je n'aime pas	I don't like	*Je voudrais ...*	I would like ...

....

....

....

....

....

....

....

....

Media

French	English	French	English
acteur/actrice	actor/actress	*les info(rmation)s*	the news
les actualités	news	*intéressant*	interesting
une ambiance	an atmosphere	*la jeunesse*	youth
le billet	ticket	*le journal*	newspaper
la boum	party	*le lendemain*	the next day
la cassette (K7)	cassette	*la maison des jeunes*	youth club
chanteur/euse	singer	*les nouvelles*	news
la chaîne	channel (TV)	*pas mal*	not bad
le cinéma	cinema	*la patinoire*	skating rink
le cirque	circus	*pendant*	during
comédien/nne	actor/actress	*le piano*	piano
comique	funny	*une place*	a seat, place
commencer	to start	*le prix*	price
la discothèque	disco	*réserver*	to book
drôle	funny	*les sous-titres*	subtitles
une émission	a programme	*le spectacle*	show
enregistrer	to record	*super*	great
l'espionnage	spying	*le théâtre*	theatre
le feuilleton	soap opera	*tout à fait*	totally
le film d'amour	love film	*un orchestre*	orchestra
le film policier	police film	*un dessin animé*	cartoon
au fond	at the back	*la vedette*	star (famous)
la guitare	guitar	*la version anglaise*	English version
Il y avait ...	there was ...	*le violon*	violin

....

....

....

....

....

Health and fitness: Parts of the body

la bouche	mouth	*la main*	hand
le bras	arm	*le nez*	nose
la dent	tooth	*un oeil/les yeux*	eye/eyes
le doigt	finger	*une oreille*	ear
le dos	back	*le pied*	foot
le genou	knee	*le sang*	blood
la gorge	throat	*la tête*	head
la jambe	leg	*le ventre*	stomach

....

....

....

....

Health and fitness: Hygiene and general well-being

avoir chaud	to be hot	*avoir froid*	to be cold
être en forme	in good health	*se maquiller*	put on make-up
avoir faim	to be hungry	*avoir mal*	to have pain
se faire mal	to hurt oneself	*aller mieux*	to be better
fatigué(e)	tired	*avoir soif*	to be thirsty

....

....

....

....

....

....

Health and fitness: Illness, injury and accident

un accident	accident	*le mal de mer*	sea sickness
un agent de police	police (person)	*le médecin*	doctor
appeler	to call	*la médecine*	medicine
attendre	to wait	*le médicament*	medicine
arrêté	arrested	*mort*	dead
s'arrêter	to stop	*mourir*	to die
Au secours!	Help!	*la naissance*	birth
avoir mal au coeur	to feel sick	*une ordonnance*	prescription
blessé	hurt	*le pansement*	bandage
se blesser	to get injured	*la pastille*	throat pastille
se brûler	to burn oneself	*le permis de conduire*	driving licence
se casser	to break	*la pharmacie*	chemist's
le comprimé	tablet	*pleurer*	to cry
le coup de soleil	sunburn	*plus tard*	later
se couper	to cut oneself	*quel dommage!*	what a pity!
la crème	cream	*le rendez-vous*	appointment
la cuillère	spoonful	*rester au lit*	stay in bed
dangereux/euse	dangerous	*le rhume*	a cold
la douleur	pain	*rouler*	to drive, roll
doucement	gently	*saigner*	to bleed
la faute	fault	*la santé*	health
la fièvre	fever	*sapeur-pompier*	fireman/woman
gonflé	swollen	*se sentir mal*	to feel ill
grave	serious	*le sirop*	medicine (syrup)
la grippe	flu	*le sparadrap*	plaster
s'inquiéter	to worry	*tomber*	to fall
une insolation	sunstroke	*tourner*	to turn
je viens de ... *(faire quelque chose)*	I have just ... (done something)	*tout à coup*	all of a sudden
les lunettes	(eye) glasses	*traverser*	to cross
le/la malade	the patient	*tué*	killed

....

....

Food and drink

un abricot	apricot	le chocolat chaud	hot chocolate
une addition	bill	le chou-fleur	cauliflower
adorer	to love	le chou	cabbage
un agneau	lamb	le citron	lemon
un ananas	pineapple	combien?	how much/many?
assez	enough	commander	to order
au lieu de	instead of	comme	like, as
aussi	also	pour commencer	to start with
avec	with	compris	included
A votre santé!	Cheers!	le concombre	cucumber
la banane	banana	la confiture	jam
le beurre	butter	les couverts	cutlery
bien cuit	well cooked	la crevette	shrimp
bien sûr	of course	les crudités	raw vegetables
la bière	beer	le dindon	turkey
le bifteck	beef steak	encore	more
le biscuit	biscuit	une entrée	main dish
le boeuf	beef	eau minérale	mineral water
boire	to drink	la fraise	strawberry
la boisson	drink	la framboise	raspberry
Bon appetit!	Enjoy your meal!	les frites	chips
le bonbon	sweet	le fromage	cheese
la bouteille	bottle	les fruits de mers	seafood
la cacahouéte	peanut	le gâteau	cake
le café	coffee	la glace	ice cream
le café (crème)	white coffee	un haricot	bean
le canard	duck	l'huile	oil
la carotte	carrot	une huître	oyster
la carte de crédit	credit card	il n'en reste plus	there is no more
ça suffit	that's enough	le jambon	ham
la cerise	cherry	le jus de fruit	fruit juice
le champignon	mushroom	le lait	milk
le chef	the cook	la limonade	lemonade
les chips	crisps	le menu	menu
le chocolat	chocolate	le menu à ... F	... franc menu

les moules	mussels	le riz	rice
la moutarde	mustard	rôti	roast
le mouton	mutton	la salade	salad, lettuce
la noisette	hazelnut	salé	salty
la noix	nut	sans	without
un oeuf	egg	satisfait	satisfied
on peut avoir...?	can we have?	le saucisson	sausage
le pain	bread	le saumon	salmon
le parfum	flavour	le sel	salt
le pâté maison	home-made pâté	serveur/euse	waiter
la pâtisserie	pastry, cakeshop	service compris	service included
la pêche	peach	servir	to serve
les petit pois	peas	seul	on its own, alone
piquant	spicy	la soupe	soup
le pique-nique	picnic	la spécialité	speciality
le plat du jour	dish of the day	le steak	steak
la poire	pear	sucré	sweet, sugary
le poisson	fish	le sucre	sugar
le poivre	pepper	pour suivre	to follow
la pomme	apple	pour terminer	to finish with
la pomme de terre	potato	le thé	tea
le porc	pork	la tomate	tomato
le poulet	chicken	tout de suite	right away
je prendrais ...	I'll have ...	la truite	trout
prendre	to take	la vanille	vanilla
préparer	to prepare	varié	varied
la prune	plum	le veau	veal
le raisin	grape	le vin	wine
la recette	recipe	vous avez choisi?	have you chosen?
une réservation	reservation	le yaourt	yoghurt

....

....

....

....

....

....

....

....

....

....

....

....

....

....

....

....

....

....

....

....

....

....

....

....

Area of Experience B: Personal and social life

 ## Identification and description

actif/active	active	*foncé*	dark (colour)
à mon avis	in my opinion	*fort*	strong
avoir l'air	to seem	*fou/folle*	crazy, mad
un an	year	*gentil/gentille*	nice, kind
un anniversaire	birthday	*gris*	grey
la barbe	beard	*heureux/euse*	happy
bavard	chatterbox	*avoir honte*	to be ashamed
beau/bel/belle	beautiful	*jaune*	yellow
bête	stupid, silly	*jeune*	young
blanc/blanche	white	*joli*	pretty
bleu	blue	*laid*	ugly
blond	fair-haired	*long/longue*	long
bouclé	wavy	*marrant*	funny, a laugh
branché	cool	*marron*	brown
bronzé	tanned	*méchant*	naughty, mean
brun	brown	*mince*	slim
le caractère	character	*nâitre*	to be born
la carte d'identité	ID card	*ne quittez pas*	don't hang up
ça s'écrit ...	it's spelt ...	*né(e)*	born
les casse-pieds	a nuisance	*noir*	black
célèbre	famous	*le nom*	name
la chance	luck	*le numéro*	number
charmant	charming	*on s'entend bien*	we get on well
les cheveux	hair	*paresseux/euse*	lazy
clair	clear (colour)	*pauvre*	poor
composer	to dial	*le pays*	country
le/la concierge	caretaker	*penser*	to think
court	short (cut)	*avoir peur*	to be afraid
croire	to believe	*plutôt*	rather
dégoûtant	disgusting	*porter*	to wear
espérer	to hope	*le prénom*	first name
étrange	strange	*raide*	straight, stiff
un étranger	foreigner	*ressembler à*	to look like
se fâcher	to get angry	*riche*	rich

rose	pink	téléphoner	to telephone
roux/rousse	red-haired	timide	shy
la rue	road	toujours	always
le sentiment	feeling	vert	green
sérieux/euse	serious	vieux/vieil/vieille	old
sportif/sportive	good at sport	la ville	town, city
sympa	nice	vraiment	truly

.... | ....

.... | ....

.... | ....

.... | ....

 ## Family, relatives, animals and pets

aîné	elder	la femme	woman, wife
un animal domestique		fiancé(e)	fiancé(e)
	pet	la fille	girl, daughter
une araignée	spider	le fils	son
le beau-père	(step) father-in-law	le frère	brother
le bébé	baby	le garçon	boy
la belle-mère	(step) mother-in-law	la grand-mère	grandmother
cadet/cadette	younger	le grand-père	grandfather
célibataire	single	la grenouille	frog
le chat	cat	un homme	man
le cheval	horse	le lapin	rabbit
la chèvre	goat	le mari	husband
le chien	dog	se marier	to marry
le cochon	pig	la mère	mother
le cochon d'Inde	guinea-pig	un oiseau	bird
le/la cousin(e)	cousin	un oncle	uncle
un demi-frère	half-brother	la perruche	budgerigar
divorcer	to divorce	les petits-enfants	grandchildren
un enfant	child	un phasme	stick insect
la famille	family	le poisson rouge	goldfish

une poule	hen		*la tante*	aunt
séparé	separated		*la tortue*	turtle, tortoise
un serpent	snake		*unique*	only (child)
la soeur	sister		*une vache*	cow
la souris	mouse		*le veuf/la veuve*	widow(er)

....

....

....

....

Free time, holidays, special occasions, making arrangements

à bientôt	see you soon		*à la campagne*	in the country
acceuillir	to welcome		*le camping*	campsite
acheter	to buy		*la carte*	map
à droite	right		*le centre commercial*	
à gauche	left			shopping centre
une agence de voyage			*le centre de vacances*	
	travel agent			holiday centre
agricole	agricultural		*le centre-ville*	town centre
à l'est	to the east		*c'était ...*	it was ...
animé	animated, lively		*le château*	castle
un appareil photo	camera		*le chemin*	the way
l'argent de poche	pocket money		*le chèque de voyage*	
un arrêt de bus	bus stop			traveller's cheque
arriver	to arrive		*la circulation*	traffic
au bord de la mer	at the seaside		*la colonie de vacances*	
au bout de	at the end of			holiday camp
une autoroute	motorway		*un concours*	a competition
la banque	bank		*continuer*	to carry on
la bienvenue	welcome		*à coté de*	beside
les bois	woods		*dans le coin*	in the area
de bonne heure	early		*danser*	to dance
			dehors	outside

économiser	to save (money)	la marée	tide
s'égarer	to get lost	marquer un but	to score a goal
une église	church	le match nul	draw (match)
un emplacement	camping plot	le monde	world
un endroit	place	la monnaie	small change
s'ennuyer	to get bored	à la montagne	in the mountains
l'environnement	environment	monter dans	get into/on
en plein air	open air	le musée	museum
ensemble	together	la musique	music
entouré de	surrounded by	la natation	swimming
une équipe	team	au nord	to the north
un espace vert	a green	on a gagné	we won
un événement	an event	on a perdu	we lost
en face de	opposite	on se voit où?	we meet where?
faire du ski	skiing	l'ouest	west
faire du vélo	cycling	en panne	broken down
faire les valises	to pack	le panneau	board, sign
la fête	festival	Pâques	Easter
les feux	traffic lights	le parapluie	umbrella
la forêt	forest	participer	to participate
gagner	to earn, win	partir en vacances	to go on holiday
gratuit	free of charge	le passe-temps	pastime, hobby
d'habitude	usually	le paysage	countryside
l'Hôtel de ville	town hall	la pêche	fishing
interdit de ...	No	la pellicule	film (camera)
la jeunesse	youth	se perdre	to get lost
jeux de société	board games	la piscine	swimming pool
jouer	to play	la plage	beach
Joyeux Noël	Happy Xmas	la planche à voile	sailboard
jusqu'à	up to, as far as	pollué	polluted
là-bas	down there	le portefeuille	wallet
libre	free, available	le porte-monnaie	purse
avoir lieu	to take place	pour aller à ...?	to get to ...?
la location	location, hire	la publicité	advertising
les loisirs	hobbies	puis	then
le long de	all along	le quartier	quarter, district
louer	to hire	la randonnée	ramble, long walk
le marché	market	rater	miss

la région	region	le syndicat d'initiative	
rendre visite à ...	to visit (person)		tourist office
les renseignements	information	le temps libre	free time
rêver	to dream	tout droit	straight on
la rivière	river	toutes directions	all directions
le rond-point	roundabout	une tente	tent
sans doute	without doubt	le terrain de sport	sports ground
le siècle	century	se trouver	to be situated
situé	situated	les vacances	holidays
si on sortait?	shall we go out?	le verglas	black ice
le ski nautique	water skiing	le virage	bend, turning
les sports d'hiver	winter sports	la voile	sailing
le stade	stadium	le voyage	journey, trip
le sud	south		

....

....

....

....

....

....

....

....

....

....

....

....

Weather

améliorer	to improve	malgré	despite
après-demain	the day after tomorrow	la météo	weather forecast
une averse	shower	la neige	snow
le brouillard	fog	il neige	it's snowing
cependant	however	neiger	to snow
la chaleur	heat	le nuage	cloud
le climat	climate	nuageux/euse	cloudy
le coucher du soleil	sunset	un orage	storm
couvert	cloudy, covered	orageux	stormy
dans ce cas	in that case	il pleut	it's raining
un éclair	lightning bolt	pleuvoir	to rain
une éclaircie	sunny spell	la pluie	rain
en plein soleil	in full sunshine	pluvieux/euse	rainy
ensoleillé	sunny	prochain	next
faire beau	to be fine	sec/sèche	dry
geler	to freeze	la sécheresse	drought
la glace	ice	le soleil	sun
grâce à	thanks to	la tempête	storm
la grêle	hail	le temps	weather
une inondation	flood	variable	variable
le lever du soleil	sunrise	le vent	wind

....

....

....

....

....

....

Area of Experience C: The world around us

 Home town, local environment and customs

la boucherie	butcher's	*la librairie*	book shop
la boulangerie	baker's	*la poissonerie*	fishmonger's
la boutique	small shop	*la poste*	post office
le cadeau	present	*la promotion*	offer
la caisse	cash desk, till	*la quincaillerie*	hardware shop
la charcuterie	pork butcher's	*le rayon*	department
le chariot	trolley	*le sac*	bag
le choix	choice	*les soldes*	sales
le coiffeur	hairdresser's	*le supermarché*	supermarket
commerçant(e)	trader	*le tabac*	tobacconist's
la confiserie	sweet shop	*vendeur/euse*	sales assistant
une épicerie	grocer's shop	*la vitrine*	shop window
le jour férié	public holiday	*le/la voleur*	thief
le libre-service	self-service		

Clothes

le blouson	bomber jacket	le jean	jeans
la ceinture	belt	la jupe	skirt
le chapeau	hat	la laine	wool
la chaussette	sock	le maillot de bain	swim suit
la chaussure	shoe	le manteau	overcoat
la chemise	shirt	la mode	fashion
le chemisier	blouse	le pantalon	pair of trousers
le collant	tights	le pull(over)	pullover
la confection	clothing (trade)	le pyjama	pyjamas
la couleur	colour	la robe	dress
la cravate	tie	le short	shorts
le cuir	leather	le slip	pants, knickers
une écharpe	scarf	la veste	jacket
les gants	gloves	les vêtements	clothes
un imperméable	raincoat		

.... | ....

.... | ....

.... | ....

.... | ....

.... | ....

.... | ....

.... | ....

.... | ....

.... | ....

.... | ....

.... | ....

Quantity, non-food items and money

à peu près	about, roughly	*ne marche pas*	does not work
l'argent	money	*moins cher*	cheaper
le billet	bank note	*multicolor*	multi-coloured
la boîte	tin, box, can	*d'occasion*	second-hand
bon marché	bargain, cheap	*le paquet*	packet
ça fait ...	that makes ...	*un peu plus*	a bit more
le carnet de chèques	cheque book	*plus ou moins*	more or less
		le pot	jar, pot
c'est pour offrir	as a gift (wrap)	*quelque*	some
essayer	to try on	*le shopping*	shopping
le kilo	kilo	*la taille*	size, height, cut
le litre	litre	*la tranche*	slice
la livre	pound	*trop*	too much
la livre sterling	pound sterling	*le trou*	hole
le morceau	bit, piece		

....

....

....

....

....

....

....

....

....

....

Services, post office, telephone, bank, lost property, repairs

s'adresser	to speak to/address	la laverie	laundrette
aucun(e)	no, none	mettre à la poste	to post
avant-hier	before yesterday	la montre	wrist watch
la batterie	car battery	le moteur	engine
le bouton	button, acne spot	le nettoyage à sec	dry cleaning
le bureau de change		le numéro	number
	exchange office	nulle part	nowhere
le cambrioleur	burglar	occupé	engaged
la carte téléphonique		objets trouvés	lost property
	phone card	par avion	by air mail
le colis	parcel	par hazard	by chance
combien de temps	how long	partout	everywhere
le courrier	mail	pas de chance	no luck
le cours de change	exchange rate	pas la peine	not worth it
crevé	punctured	le passeport	passport
déchirer	to tear	passer à la caisse	go to cash desk
décrire	to describe	en PCV	reversed charges
les douanes	customs (office)	la pièce	coin
emprunter	to borrow	la pile	battery
entendre	to hear	le plombier	plumber
envoyer	to send	prêt	ready
en espèces	in cash	PTT	post office
à l'étranger	abroad	qui	who
le facteur	postman	rappeler	call back
le frein	the break	rembourser	to reimburse
le guichet	counter window	remplacer	to replace
ici	here	remplir une fiche	fill in a form
il faut ...	it is necessary to	rendre	to give back
il s'agit de ...	it's about ...	la réparation	a repair
j'ai perdu	I've lost	retrouver	to find
je l'ai laissé(e)	I left it	la roue	wheel
laisser	to leave, let	le sac à main	handbag
laisser tomber	to drop	le tarif	price list
la marque	brand name	le timbre	stamp
large	broad, wide	la tonalité	dialing tone

toucher un chèque	cash a cheque	*vérifier*	to check
tout neuf	brand new	*vide*	empty
la valise	suitcase	*le vol*	theft, flight

Public transport and service stations

un aérogliseur	hovercraft	les papiers	documents
un aller-retour	return ticket	le pare-brise	windscreen
un aller simple	single ticket	payant	paying
annoncer	to announce	le péage	toll
une arrivée	arrival	le phare	headlight
le bagage	luggage	le pneu	tyre
le billet	ticket	le poids lourd	HGV, heavy lorry
Bon voyage!	Have a good trip!	le/la pompiste	pump attendant
le camion	truck	première classe	1st class
la camionette	van	priorité à droite	priority to right
le car	coach	en provenance de	coming from
le car-ferry	car ferry	prochain	next
le casque	helmet	le quai	platform
circuler	to move about	quelque chose	something
composter	punch ticket	la route nationale	major road
contrôler	to check	le salle d'attente	waiting room
décoller	to take off	le sans plomb	unleaded petrol
dernier	last	la SNCF	French railways
le départ	departure	la sortie	exit
deuxième classe	2nd class	stationner	to park
un embouteillage	traffic jam	tomber en panne	to break down
l'essence	petrol	les travaux	roadworks
faites-le plein!	fill it up!	la traversée	crossing
fumeur	smoking	vendez-vous ...?	do you sell ...?
le gazole	diesel	la vitesse	speed
un horaire	timetable	la voie	track
il me faut ...	I need ...	le volant	steering wheel
lent	slow	voler	to fly
mécanicien/ienne	car mechanic	le voyageur	traveller
obligatoire	compulsory	le wagon	wagon

....

....

....

Area of Experience D: The world of work

 Further education and training, careers and employment

j'aimerais ...	I'd like to ...		*la femme au foyer*	housewife
l'armée de l'air	Air Force		*la femme d'affaires*	business woman
bien payé	well paid		*infirmier/ière*	nurse
boucher/bouchère	butcher		*jardinier/ière*	gardener
boulanger/ère	baker		*je vais être ...*	I'm going to be ...
chirurgien/ienne	surgeon		*le/la journaliste*	journalist
le chômage	unemployment		*maçon/maçonne*	bricklayer
coiffeur/euse	hairdresser		*mal payé*	badly paid
le/la comptable	accountant		*le métier*	occupation, job
cuisinier/ière	cook		*le poste*	position, job
un emploi	job		*la profession*	profession
employé(e)	employee		*le professeur*	teacher
être attiré(e) par	I'm drawn to ...		*le/la secrétaire*	secretary
les études	studies		*un travail varié*	a varied job
étudiant(e)	student			

....

....

....

....

....

....

....

....

....

Area of Experience E: The international world

 Life in other countries, tourism, accommodation

apporter	to bring	*le linge*	linen, washing
appuyer	to push, press	*ne marche(nt) pas*	do(es)n't work
un aubèrge	hostel	*nul/nulle*	terrible
un avantage	advantage	*pas cher*	not expensive
camper	to camp	*la pension complète*	full board
la chasse	hunting	*le plan de ville*	street map
complet	full	*pousser/poussez*	push
la place	space, place	*la prise de courrant*	power point
donner sur	to overlook (view)	*privé*	private
eau potable	drinking water	*la réception*	reception
faire du camping	to go camping	*le sac de couchage*	sleeping bag
le gîte	holiday home	*la salle de jeux*	games room
un incendie	a fire (outbreak)	*le silence*	silence
un inconvénient	disadvantage	*toute l'année*	all year round
la lessive	washing powder		

Countries, nationalities and people

Country		Adjective	Inhabitant
l'Europe	Europe	européen/enne	Européen/enne
l'Allemagne	Germany	allemand(e)	Allemand(e)
l'Angleterre	England	anglais(e)	Anglais(e)
La Grande Bretagne	Great Britain	britannique	Britannique
le Royaume-Uni	United Kingdom		
la Belgique	Belgium	belge	Belge
le Canada	Canada	canadien(ne)	Canadien/enne
le Danemark	Denmark	danois(e)	Danois(e)
l'Espagne	Spain	espagnol(e)	Espagnol(e)
la France	France	français(e)	Français(e)
la Grèce	Greece	grec/greque	Grec/Greque
la Hollande	Holland	hollandais(e)	Hollandais(e)
les Pays Bas	Netherlands	néerlandais(e)	Néerlandais(e)
l'Italie	Italy	italien(ne)	Italien/enne
le Luxembourg	Luxembourg	luxembourgeois(e)	Luxembourgeois(e)
le Portugal	Portugal	portugais(e)	Portugais(e)
la Suisse	Switzerland	suisse	Suisse
l'Amérique	America	américain(e)	Américain(e)
les États-Unis	USA		
la Chine	China	chinois(e)	Chinois(e)
l'Écosse	Scotland	écossais(e)	Écossais(e)
l'Inde	India	indien(ne)	Indien(ne)
l'Irlande	Ireland	irlandais(e)	Irlandais(e)
l'Irlande du Nord	Northern Ireland	irlandais(e)	Irlandais(e)
le Japon	Japan	japonais(e)	Japonais(e)
le Pays de Galles	Wales	gallois(e)	Gallois(e)
la Russie	Russia	russe	Russe

.... | ....

.... | ....

.... | ....

.... | ....

World events

à cause de	because of		un immigré	immigrant
une actualité	piece of news		un impôt	tax
augmenter	to increase		la maladie	disease
le catastrophe	disaster		menacé	threatened
la couche d'ozone	ozone layer		la nourriture	food
le développement	development		nucléaire	nuclear
diminuer	to diminish		la pauvreté	poverty
la disparition	disappearing		la politique	politics, policy
l'effet de serre	greenhouse effect		le premier ministre	Prime Minister
l'énergie	energy		le président	President
une époque	time period		le réchauffement	warming (global)
une espèce	species		la reine	queen
la faim	hunger, famine		le roi	king
la forêt tropicale	rainforest		le SIDA	AIDS
le gouvernement	government		le syndicat	trade union
la grève	strike		le Tiers Monde	Third World
la guerre	war		la violence	violence
l'habitat	habitat			

....

....

....

....

His French vocabulary was rapidly approaching double figures...

7 La France

This map of France shows the regions:

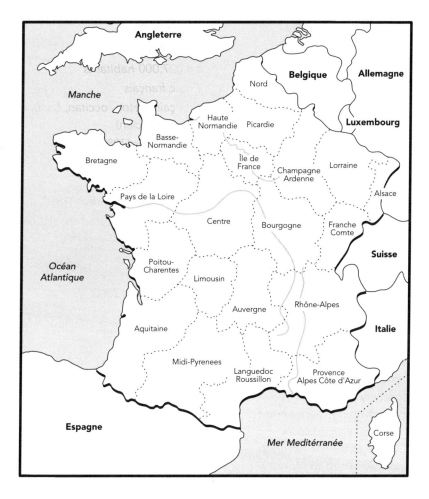

Find out where the following towns are and mark them on the map:

- Bordeaux
- Calais
- Lille
- Lyon
- Paris
- Strasbourg
- Caen
- Dijon
- Limoges
- Marseille
- Rennes
- Toulouse

French facts

Capitale	Paris (2,152,000 habitants)
Villes principales	Lyon (1,262,000)
	Marseille (1,230,000)
	Lille (959,000)
Superficie	547,000 km^2
Population	58,027,000 habitants
Monnaie	Franc français
Langues	Français (beton, occitan, basque, corse, alsacien)
Religions	Catholiques (72%)
	Musulmans (8%)
	Juifs (2%)
	Sans religion et autres (18%)
Fête nationale	14 juillet (date d'anniversaire de la prise de la Bastille, 1789)
Chef de l'État	Jacques Chirac

Présidence du Conseil de l'UE: 2ème semestre 2000

L'Hexagone

Since, with a bit of imagination, the map of the country fits into an approximate shape, France is often referred to as l'Hexagone. The hexagon shape is used to represent France in many graphic designs.

There are more sides to me than six!

French handwriting

French students are taught to start their joined-up letters from the bottom line. This means that to write a letter that would normally start at the top in English, they have to firstly draw a line from the bottom up to the top where they will start to form the letter. This gives many letters an extra line!

Letters that are usually vertical lines in English, often have a loop at the top, and can cause confusion:

Some letters appear in two or three different ways depending on the writer's style, which can also be confusing:

To avoid confusion over accents going one way or the other, French students often combine the two. Sneaky… but effective!

Ask your teacher about getting a French-speaking pen-pal. This is a great way to get to know the people and the country as well as getting a lot of practice at reading French handwriting.

I'm sorry, I can't understand your accent...

Going to France

The day trip

Since France is only about 20 miles away at its nearest point, the English Channel can quickly be crossed by hovercraft, ferry or Channel-tunnel train, but the crossing is only part of your journey. Day trips can be very rewarding as well as very tiring. Start by asking yourself a few questions:

- **Why has this trip been planned?** – The National Curriculum Programme of Study, Part 1, insists that students should be given opportunities to 'come into contact with native speakers in this country and, where possible, abroad'. It is hoped that trips to France will provide positive experiences that will encourage you to keep learning French or at least feel good about the subject. Most teachers are motivated by their love of the language and its people and they hope that some

of this will rub off on those they teach. So, if you thought you were just going to have a good time with a bunch of your school mates – you're right! Only your teacher's idea of a good time might not be exactly what you had in mind, but at least give them the chance to prove to you that it can be fun learning French.

- **How prepared am I for the opportunities this trip provides?** – Your teachers will be hoping that you will use the French you have learned in class, so think about what opportunities you might have to speak French and look up the relevant vocabulary and phrases. Your teacher will be only too pleased to talk to you about words you might need in a 'real' situation. It is all too easy to sit back and hope 'they all speak English!' Even if they can, why should they?

- **How will this trip affect my learning of French?** – One of the unknown quantities in planning any trip to France is how the experience will affect the language learning of the classroom. The greatest effect is usually an increased confidence in the students' performance. Students who have been on trips, and have tried their best to learn from them, are usually more enthusiastic and prepared to 'have a go' than they were before their experience in France.

  You will be the main factor in determining the effect of your trip(s) to France. If you make the most of the opportunities to use the language you are trying to learn, you will find that your confidence grows and your understanding will seem to quicken as a result.

- **Will this experience be positive?** – Like all experiences in life, a trip to France can be 'positive' or 'negative', or even somewhere in between. You are more likely to enjoy the trip if the people in charge are smiling and happy! By following the instructions and responding sensitively to the leaders of your group, you will avoid the backlash of a frayed temper or a short fuse. Read the rules and regulations issued by your teacher and expect to follow them.

- **Passports and documentation** – For any trip to France, you will need a passport, insurance and, depending on your nationality, maybe even a visa. These documents need to be arranged well in advance of your trip. They take time to arrange so don't put it off!

The short-stay holiday

These trips avoid the anxieties associated with staying in a French family and tend to foster more enthusiasm than an exchange, where you might have to speak to French people.

Since you will spend nearly all of your time together as a group – probably speaking English – the linguistic challenge is far easier to avoid than on a student exchange. Asking yourself the same questions as for the day trip (see previous page) will increase your chances of making an impact on your learning of the French language.

Excursions and visits to places of interest will be arranged to add breadth to your experience and give you a greater insight into the French culture and way of life. Be prepared to give each visit a chance.

An otherwise long and boring coach journey can become a revision class, if you take notes from signs, billboards or posters you see.

If that's how you feel, I'm off...

French exchange

The emphasis on GCSE examination success can often focus very heavily on presenting yourself and telling someone all about you. This proves to be of very limited value on a French exchange, and students often wish that they had spent more time learning how to talk about other things, such as television programmes, films, pop stars, football teams and the like. To be in a good position to join in with more of the conversations you will hear on the French exchange, be sure and learn the vocabulary and the expressions that will help you do this.

One of the best preparations for a French exchange is to speak only French in the classroom. The more you get used to trying to say what you want, what you need, or what you think about something, the more likely you are to realise how the French words and phrases that you are learning can be used in a whole range of contexts and for a wide variety of purposes. If you cannot say what you need to in French, learn how to, and practise it for next time! Ask yourself, 'How many times have I spoken French in class today?'

The best French exchanges are when there is a good relationship between the students and the host families. This might happen purely by chance, but more often than not it is because of the social skills of the students involved. To practice this, vary your working partners for pair and group work. If you can survive a short classroom activity with someone without complaining, then you will be all the more likely to manage your exchange experience.

The more you build a relationship with your partner through letters, phone calls or email, the more likely you are to be able to anticipate what you might be talking about when you meet.

A few tips to help make your exchange trip run smoothly:

- Contact your partner and the host family before the exchange.

- When packing for your exchange remember that you are only going for a short while and you do not need to take your entire wardrobe. Take clothes suited to the activities in which you will be involved. You will be doing a lot of walking so think about your feet too!

- Presents are traditionally part of the exchange experience. Typically English presents, things that you cannot easily find in France, are usually appreciated – marmalade, decorated tins of sweets, biscuits or English teas, teapots, small pieces of Wedgewood or similar English crafted items.

- Make an effort to stay with your partner whenever you are supposed to and be sure to talk to them.

- Be prepared to participate in the activities that have been planned for you, but don't be afraid to say if there are things you really do not want to do.

- Make up your mind that you will try French food before you refuse it. One of the greatest worries that exchange families have is that the partner is not eating properly. Try not to cause anxiety.

- Don't shut yourself away in your room all the time. Let the host family see you, and see you smiling.

- Try to avoid grouping up with others unless you are prepared to include the French partners.

- Speak with your teachers about anything that is upsetting you as soon as it does.

- Always be punctual, polite and patient.

Work experience in France

Work experience in France may be a possibility during post-16 studies. Your school careers advisor will be able to pass on information about possible funding through organisations in Europe whose aim is to promote such exchanges.

Answers

Exercise A (page 26)

The following are nouns: 3 stylo,
4 chat, 5 mére, 6 gomme, 8 livre,
9 silence, 10 table, 11 crayon.

Exercise B (page 27)

1 le, 2 le, 3 le, 4 la, 5 la, 6 la, 7 le,
8 le, 9 les, 10 la, 11 la, 12 l' (f).

Exercise C (page 28)

1 une, 2 un, 3 un, 4 un, 5 une,
6 une, 7 une, 8 une, 9 un, 10 une, 11
un, 12 un.

Exercise D (page 28)

1 journaux, 2 chevaux, 3 neveux,
4 eaux, 5 nez, 6 prix, 7 tables,
8 crayons.

Exercise E (page 29)

1 de la, 2 du, 3 du, 4 du, 5 du, 6 du,
7 du, 8 du, 9 de la, 10 de la, 11 de l',
12 de la.

Exercise F (page 29)

Je ne mange pas... 1 de bonbons,
2 de yaourt, 3 de viande,
4 de poisson, 5 de chocolat,
6 de soupe, 7 de pizza, 8 de riz.

Exercise A (page 31)

1 Tu, 2 Vous, 3 Tu, 4 Vous, 5 Vous,
6 Tu, 7 Vous, 8 Tu.

Exercise B (page 31)

1 Ils, 2 Elles, 3 Elles, 4 Elles, 5 Elles,
6 Ils, 7 Ils, 8 Elles, 9 Ils, 10 Ils,
11 Ils, 12 Ils.

Exercise C (page 32)

1 On va au café. 2 Ici, nous parlons
français. 3 On mange beaucoup.
4 On peut entrer? 5 Nous allons à la
plage. 6 Nous allons bientôt arriver.

Exercise D (page 32)

1 me, 2 her, 3 the cat, 4 an apple,
5 a car, 6 you.

Exercise E (page 33)

1 Il le voit. 2 Je l'aime. 3 Elle le voit.
4 Il me trouve. 5 Je le cherche.
6 Ils nous trouvent.

Exercise F (page 33)

1 l', 2 les, 3 la, 4 m', 5 les.

Exercise G (page 34)

1 her, 2 him, 3 me, 4 him, 5 me, 6
them, 7 them, 8 you.

Exercise H (page 35)

1 lui, 2 me, 3 nous, 4 t', 5 leur, 6 lui.

Exercise I (page 35)

1 it (direct), him (indirect),
2 story (direct), them (indirect),
3 a car (direct), him (indirect),
4 postcard (direct), me (indirect),
5 letter (direct), you (indirect),
6 tie-pin (direct), him (indirect).

Exercise J (page 36)

1 Marie me les prête. 2 Vous nous les
achetez. 3 Le prof les lui donne.
4 Je te la donne. 5 Elle la leur donne.
6 Papa vous les achète.

Answers

Exercise K (page 36)
1 Elle la lui envoie. 2 Nous le lui achetons. 3 Je le lui ai acheté. 4 Nous les leur avons donnés.

Exercise L (page 37)
1 lui, 2 nous, 3 elle, 4 eux, 5 lui, 6 elles.

Exercise M (page 37)
1 Qui, 2 Que, 3 Qui, 4 Que, 5 Qui, 6 Qu'est-ce que.

Exercise N (page 39)
1 Que, 2 Qui, 3 Qui, 4 Que, 5 Qui, 6 Qui.

Exercise O (page 39)
1 J'y vais. 2 Tu en veux encore? 3 Mon père y travaille. 4 Il en a deux. 5 Nous y sommes. 6 Paul m'en a parlé.

Exercise A (page 40)
1 fine, 2 noisy, 3 little, 4 tired, 5 cold, 6 big, black, 7 nice, a bit shy, 8 easy.

Exercise B (page 41)
1 Une jolie fille. 2 Un bon élève. 3 Un joli petit village. 4 Un petit lapin noir. 5 Une maison moderne. 6 Un long voyage. 7 Un mauvais prof. 8 Des chaussettes blanches. 9 Une bonne idée. 10 Une vieille dame.

Exercise C (page 41)
1 Je l'ai fait de mes propres mains. 2 C'est la seule solution. 3 Il y a une réunion des anciens élèves. 4 Un pull cher en laine. 5 Either, depending on meaning, 'These poor people!' or 'Poor people'.

Exercise D (page 42)
1 grande, 2 lourd, 3 jolie, 4 bruyant, 5 branchée, 6 petite, 7 noire, 8 étroite, 9 bavard, 10 chaude.

Exercise E (page 44)
1 bavardes, 2 modernes, 3 petite, 4 fausse, 5 première, 6 marron, 7 malade, 8 petits, 9 vieille, 10 grecque, 11 blanche, 12 blonds.

Exercise F (page 45)
a 1 Mon, 2 Mon, 3 Mes, 4 Mon, 5 Mes, 6 Mes, 7 Ma, 8 Ma, 9 Mon, 10 Ma, 11 Mes, 12 Mes.

b 1 Tes, 2 Ton, 3 Tes, 4 Tes, 5 Tes, 6 Ta, 7 Tes, 8 Ta, 9 Ton, 10 Ton, 11 Ta, 12 Tes.

c 1 Ses, 2 Ses, 3 Son, 4 Son, 5 Son, 6 Ses, 7 Sa, 8 Sa, 9 Son, 10 Sa, 11 Sa, 12 Son.

d 1 Notre, 2 Nos, 3 Nos, 4 Nos, 5 Notre, 6 Notre, 7 Notre, 8 Nos.

e 1 Vos, 2 Vos, 3 Votre, 4 Votre, 5 Vos, 6 Vos, 7 Vos, 8 Votre.

f 1 leurs, 2 leur, 3 leur, 4 leur, 5 leurs, 6 leurs, 7 leurs, 8 leur.

Exercise G (page 46)
1 Quelle, 2 Quels, 3 Quelles, 4 Quels, 5 Quel, 6 Quelle, 7 Quelle, 8 Quelle.

Exercise H (page 47)
1 Ce, 2 Cette, 3 Ce, 4 Ces, 5 Cet, 6 Cet, 7 Cette, 8 Cet.

Exercise I (page 47)
1 plus fort, 2 plus grande, 3 moins intelligent, 4 aussi douée, 5 moins chère.

Exercise J (page 47)

1 plus grand que, 2 moins grande que, 3 aussi grande que, 4 plus grand que, 5 moins grande que, 6 aussi grand que.

Exercise K (page 48)

1 meilleur que, moins cher, 2 la plus haute, 3 meilleure, 4 bon, le meilleur, 5 meilleur.

Exercise A (page 49)

1 hate, 2 arrived, 3 ringing, 4 like, 5 is, 6 are, 7 chased, 8 says, 9 is, 10 is watching.

Exercise B (page 49)

1 to meet, 2 to ask, 3 to drive, 4 to teach, 5 to walk, 6 to recognise, 7 to draw, 8 to choose, 9 to know, 10 to see, 11 to drink, 12 to tick.

Exercise C (page 52)

1 regardes, 2 aimez, 3 porte, 4 arrive, 5 travailles, 6 danse, 7 détestent, 8 jouent, 9 habitons, 10 parle.

Exercise D (page 53)

1 finis, 2 réussissent, 3 choisis, 4 finissez, 5 remplit, 6 grossit, 7 sortez, 8 partons, 9 dors, 10 repart, 11 sentent, 12 pars.

Exercise E (page 54)

1 descendez, 2 attendons, 3 descend, 4 vend, 5 vends, 6 répondent, 7 attends, 8 attends.

Exercise F (page 55)

1 Ils se lavent. 2 Vous vous habillez. 3 Il se douche. 4 Nous nous réveillons. 5 Tu te lèves. 6 Je me lave.

Exercise G (page 56)

1 ai, 2 allez, 3 a, 4 sont, 5 as, 6 es, 7 avons, 8 va, 9 sommes, 10 vais.

Exercise H (page 58)

1 imperfect – describing feelings, 2 perfect – happened only once, 3 perfect – happened only once, 4 perfect – happened only once, 5 imperfect – background/were ...ing, 6 perfect – can say exactly when, 7 perfect – happened only once, 8 imperfect – happened frequently, 9 perfect – happened only once/can say exactly when, 10 imperfect – used to.

Exercise I (page 59)

1 was ringing (imperfect), I came in (perfect), 2 was watching (imperfect), I left (perfect), 3 I wanted (imperfect), she said (perfect), 4 She was very tired (imperfect), she arrived (perfect), 5 I discovered (perfect), I was five (imperfect), I wore (imperfect).

Exercise J (page 62)

1 ai, 2 avons, 3 est, 4 sont, 5 est, 6 as, 7 a, 8 ont.

Exercise K (page 62)

1 est descendu, 2 a entendu, 3 a eu, 4 a pris, 5 avez écouté, 6 a mangé, 7 avons fait, 8 ai lu.

Exercise L (page 63)

1 s'est couchée, 2 vous êtes réveillé(e)s, 3 s'est habillé, 4 se sont disputés, 5 nous sommes levé(e)s, 6 t'es lavé?, 7 s'est approché, 8 s'est ennuyées.

Answers

Exercise M (page 64)

1 jouait, 2 écoutais, 3 étaient,
4 voulaient, 5 avais, 6 attendions,
7 regardait, 8 était, 9 faisait, 10 lisiez.

Exercise N (page 64)

Je suis allé, Je suis allé, je voulais, était,
il faisait beau, j'avais, j'ai pris, je suis
descendu, je faisais, j'ai vu, je cherchais,
je suis entré, je l'ai acheté, était.

Exercise A (page 65)

1 vais faire, 2 vas rester, 3 allez jouer,
4 va prendre, 5 vont dormir, 6 vont
écouter, 7 va travailler, 8 vont sortir,
9 allons regarder, 10 va gagner.

Exercise B (page 66)

1 arriveras, 2 finira, 3 achetera,
4 mangeront, 5 retournerai,
6 sortirons.

Exercise C (page 67)

1 aurai, 2 pourront, 3 saurons, 4 ira,
5 seront, 6 feras, 7 verez, 8 sera,
9 fera, 10 devrez.

Exercise A (page 68)

1 resterais, 2 serait, 3 pourraient,
4 voudrais, 5 pourrais, 6 prendrait.

Exercise A (page 69)

1 Elle ne regarde pas. 2 Elles
n'écoutent pas. 3 Nous n'allons pas.
4 Ils n'habitent pas. 5 Je ne joue pas.
6 On ne mange pas. 7 Vous ne
travaillez pas. 8 ne vient pas.

Exercise B (page 69)

1 Je ne suis pas allé. 2 Il n'est pas
resté à la maison. 3 Vous n'avez pas
téléphoné. 4 Marie et Claire ne sont
pas arrivées. 5 Nous n'avons pas joué
au tennis. 6 Tu n'es pas parti sans elle.
7 Paul n'a pas fait du vélo. 8 Elles
n'ont pas travaillé.

Exercise C (page 70)

1 Je ne suis jamais allé. 2 Il n'attend
personne. 3 Tu n'as rien gagné.
4 Elles n'ont qu'un franc. 5 Nous ne
jouons plus au tennis. 6 Tu ne bois ni
café ni thé. 7 Paul n'a fait que du vélo.
8 Ils ne sont jamais arrivés.

Exercise A (page 71)

1 vite, 2 doucement, 3 absolument,
4 bien, 5 normalment, 6 mal.

Exercise A (page 72)

1 à la, 2 au, 3 à, 4 au, 5 à, 6 à la, 7 au,
8 au Mans, 9 à.

Exercise B (page 73)

1 du, 2 de, 3 de, 4 de, 5 des, 6 de la,
7 d', 8 de la, 9 de, 10 de.